D0657342

DIVORCE

FAMILY STUDIES TEXT SERIES

Series Editor: RICHARD J. GELLES, *University of Rhode Island*
Series Associate Editor: ALEXA A. ALBERT, *University of Rhode Island*

This series of textbooks is designed to examine topics relevant to a broad view of family studies. The series is aimed primarily at undergraduate students of family sociology and family relations, among others. Individual volumes will be useful to students in psychology, home economics, counseling, human services, social work, and other related fields. Core texts in the series cover such subjects as theory and conceptual design, research methods, family history, cross-cultural perspectives, and life course analysis. Other texts will cover traditional topics, such as dating and mate selection, parenthood, divorce and remarriage, and family power. Topics that have been receiving more recent public attention will also be dealt with, including family violence, later life families, and fatherhood.

Because of their wide range and coverage, Family Studies Texts can be used singly or collectively to supplement a standard text or to replace one. These books will be of interest to both students and professionals in a variety of disciplines.

Volumes in this series:

1. LATER LIFE FAMILIES, Timothy H. Brubaker

2. INTIMATE VIOLENCE IN FAMILIES,
   Richard J. Gelles & Claire Pedrick Cornell

3. BECOMING A PARENT, Ralph LaRossa

4. FAMILY RESEARCH METHODS, Brent C. Miller

5. PATHS TO MARRIAGE, Bernard I. Murstein

6. WORK AND FAMILY LIFE, Patricia Voydanoff

7. REMARRIAGE, Marilyn Ihinger-Tallman & Kay Pasley

8. FAMILY STRESS MANAGEMENT, Pauline Boss

9. DIVORCE, Sharon J. Price & Patrick C. McKenry

10. FAMILIES AND HEALTH, William J. Doherty & Thomas L. Campbell

Sharon J. Price
and
Patrick C. McKenry

DIVORCE

FAMILY STUDIES
TEXT SERIES 9

To the children in our lives . . .

> *Wendy Price*
> *Christine Price*
> *Steven Coker*
>
> *John McKenry*
> *Adam McKenry*
> *Michael McKenry*

Copyright © 1988 by Sage Publications, Inc.

For information address:

SAGE Publications, Inc.
2111 West Hillcrest Drive
Newbury Park, California 91320

SAGE Publications Inc.
275 South Beverly Drive
Beverly Hills
California 90212

SAGE Publications Ltd.
28 Banner Street
London EC1Y 8QE
England

SAGE PUBLICATIONS India Pvt. Ltd.
M-32 Market
Greater Kailash I
New Delhi 110 048 India

Printed in the United States of America

Library of Congress Cataloging-in-Publication Data

Price, Sharon J.
    Divorce / Sharon J. Price, Patrick C. McKenry.
        p.   cm.—(Family studies text series ; v. 9)
    Bibliography: p.
    Includes index.
    ISBN 0-8039-2356-2   ISBN 0-8039-2357-0 (pbk.)
    1. Divorce—United States.   I. McKenry, Patrick C.   II. Title.
    III. Series.
    HQ834.P75 1987
    306.8'9'0973—dc19   87-26959
                                                    CIP

FIRST PRINTING 1988

CONTENTS

Acknowledgments 6

Introduction 7

1. Divorce in Societal Context 8

2. Why People Divorce 21

3. Separation 36

4. Adjusting to Divorce 55

5. Children and Divorce 73

6. Legal Aspects of Divorce 91

7. Economics of Divorce 107

8. Intervention and Divorce 124

References 140

Author Index 155

Subject Index 158

About the Authors 160

ACKNOWLEDGMENTS

THE AUTHORS WOULD LIKE TO EXPRESS their appreciation to everyone who helped produce this volume. In particular, we would like to acknowledge Dr. John Crosby, University of Kentucky, Dr. Helen Raschke, West Texas Legal Services, and Dr. David Wright, Kansas State University, for their very thoughtful reviews; Dr. Lena Bailey and Dr. Barbara Newman, Ohio State University, for their continuing support of this project; Dr. James Walters, University of Georgia, for his warmth and support; Dr. Anne Sweaney for her assistance; graduate assistants Patty Dedrick, Teresa Julian, and James Kuo; and our secretaries and manuscript assistants, Dawn Ball, Elizabeth Ratcliff, Judith Strain, and Sarah Twitty. And a special thank you to DLC.

INTRODUCTION

THIS COUNTRY WITNESSED A PRECIPITOUS increase in divorce during the 1970s that stabilized in the 1980s. The refined divorce rate increased from 10.6 per 1,000 married women 15 years of age and older in 1965 to 22.8 in 1979, and stabilized in the 1980s at around 22 divorces per 1,000 married women 15 years of age and older. Furthermore, it is projected that 40% of all persons born in the 1970s and who marry will divorce. Several factors have contributed to this increase: (1) increased education and employment of women, (2) fewer children in families, (3) economic affluence, (4) free legal aid, (5) the Vietnam War, (6) greater social and religious acceptance of divorce, (7) reform of divorce laws, (8) growth and age distribution of married persons, and (9) emphasis on individualism.

Prior to the last decade, and compared to other family phenomena, there was a paucity of systematic research or theoretical work on divorce. Seminal studies included J. P. Lichtenberger's in 1909, Willard Waller's in 1930, and William Goode's (1956) study of divorced women. The recent increase in divorce, however, has been accompanied by a similar increase in interest by social scientists. This is evidenced by the number of articles on divorce published in professional journals, the establishment of a journal devoted almost exclusively to divorce, the *Journal of Divorce,* and several research-based books on the topic. Recent studies that have significantly contributed to our understanding of the divorce process include, among others, research conducted by Bernard Bloom, Gay Kitson, Mavis Hetherington, Graham Spanier, Judith Wallerstein and Joan Kelly, George Levinger, Lenore Weitzman and Constance Ahrons.

In addition, books on how to initiate and survive divorce have challenged sex manuals in popularity, divorce insurance is discussed, divorce greeting cards are available, and organizations that offer counsel and support to divorcing/divorced persons are increasingly common. This heightened interest is also evident in the American popular culture; divorce is a recurrent theme in movies (e.g., *An Unmarried Woman, Kramer vs. Kramer, Starting Over,* and *Twice in a Lifetime*), and TV shows often include divorce-related themes (e.g., *Golden Girls* and *Falcon Crest*).

For the purpose of this book, divorce is defined as the legal dissolution of a socially and legally recognized marital relationship that alters the obligations and privileges of the two persons involved. It is also a major life transition that has far-reaching social, psychological, legal, personal, economic, and parental consequences.

CHAPTER

1

Divorce in Societal Context

Suddenly divorce seems to be all around you. Even the President of the United States is divorced, with a set of children from each marriage. You go to the movies and see *Starting Over, An Unmarried Woman* and *Shoot the Moon*. You watch the *Last Married Couple in America* on Home Box Office. You turn on the radio and hear the country music classic: "D-I-V-O-R-C-E." Whatever happened to "I Can't Give You Anything But Love" and "Someone to Watch Over Me." Now the themes of love have changed from the sixties. "Chains, My Baby's Got Me Locked Up in Chains" to "Upside Down, Boy You Turn Me Inside Out, and Round and Round" of the eighties. The old myths and manners of marriage are gone.[Trafford, 1982: xiii]

PROBABLY NO OTHER FAMILY ISSUE has elicited as much societal concern as divorce. Divorce statistics have often been used to substantiate the claim that the family system is in a state of breakdown and decay. Yet, by understanding the cultural and historical context in which divorce occurs, examining how divorce rates are computed, and focusing on social patterns of divorce, it is less than clear that divorce rates constitute a valid measure of the present state of marriages and families (Crosby, 1980).

DIVORCE IN CROSS-CULTURAL
AND HISTORICAL PERSPECTIVE

The preoccupation of American society with current divorce rates often obscures the fact that some form of marital dissolution exists in all societies. By examining divorce rates in cross-cultural and historical perspectives, the universal and even functional nature of this phenomenon is readily apparent; also, present divorce rates in the United States appear modest in contrast.

8

Cross-Cultural Perspective

Contrary to common assumption, high divorce rates are not unique to the United States. Although this country currently has the highest divorce rate among major industrialized nations (see Table 1.1), other nations have had as high or higher rates at various times throughout history. Furthermore, divorce rates have risen in most nations over the course of the twentieth century as a result of industrialization and urbanization.

In a classic study of 40 non-European societies (essentially small and preliterate), Murdock (1950) found that all but one had some provision for dissolving marriages, and in approximately 60% of these nations, the marital dissolution rates were found, at that time, to exceed the rate in the United States. Even today, in many tribal communities in India, divorce is accomplished simply by an individual publicly walking up to a man or woman other than his or her spouse. And in some polygamous Moslem societies, where divorce rates have been extremely high, a man can divorce one of his wives simply by repeating before witnesses "I divorce you" three times (Dyer, 1983; Hutter, 1981). In societies where divorce is difficult to obtain, there is a tendency toward dishonest annulment, fabrication of legally accepted offenses, migratory divorce, and legal separations; divorce thus universally exists de facto, if not in fact. For example, until recently divorce in France was often an orchestrated masquerade in which the two principal parties, the lawyers, and the judge were forced to collaborate in order to circumvent existing law. This included writing false, abusive letters. Under Napoleonic civil code, the guilt of one of the spouses had to be determined even if both spouses desired the divorce (Robertson, 1975; cited in Hutter, 1981).

The universal existence of marital dissolution across societies is viewed by social scientists as functional rather than reflecting either personal failure or the failure of the family institution itself. Almost no society, however, places a positive value on divorce. Divorce is viewed as an *escape valve*—a way out of a dysfunctional marriage.

The viability of divorce as an escape valve can be seen in those societies that make divorce extremely difficult. Blake (1962) in Adams (1986) graphically illustrates potential negative consequences for societies with restrictive divorce laws in the following nineteenth-century Indian legend:

> In the first year of the reign of King Julief, two thousand married couples separated, by the magistrates, with their own consent. The emperor was so indignant, on learning these particulars, that he abolished the privilege of divorce. In the course of the following year, the number of marriages in

TABLE 1.1
Crude Divorce Rates[a] in Major Industrialized Nations: 1983

United States	5.04	Sweden	2.40
USSR	3.47	Netherlands	2.27
West Germany	2.97	France	1.71
United Kingdom	2.94	Japan	1.38
Denmark	2.89	Israel	1.20
Australia	2.77	Italy	0.22

SOURCE: Demographic Yearbook (1985)
a. Ratio of the number of divorces for each 1,000 persons in the population.

Agra was less than before by three thousand; the number of adulteries was greater by seven thousand; three hundred women were burned alive for poisoning their husbands; seventy-five men were burned for the murder of their wives; and the quantity of furniture broken and destroyed, in the interior of private families, amounted to the value of three millions of rupees. The emperor reestablished the privilege of divorce. [p. 329]

Also, it should be observed that high divorce rates do not necessarily reflect societal decay. For example, high divorce rates were common in many Arab Islamic societies for centuries, yet they were not related to negative societal change. Murdock (1950) concluded the that "despite the widespread alarm about increasing family disorganization in our society, the comparative evidence makes it clear that we shall remain within the limits that human experience has shown that societies can tolerate with safety" (p. 197). High divorce rates also appear not to be related to societal disillusionment with the institution of marriage. Instead, studies of recent increases in divorce rates in Europe, for example, suggest that high divorce rates are related to an idealized view of marriage and acceptance of remarriage as a viable union (Chester, 1977).

Historical Perspective

The early American settlers were primarily religiously devout Protestants. They brought with them not only New Testament resistance to divorce, but also Old Testament patriarchal values that supported stable family life (Gettleman and Markowitz, 1974). For many years, the Church of England had full authority to enforce its view of marriage as a sacrament that could not be broken, for example, "those whom God hath joined together, let no man put asunder." The legal conception of marriage was thus bound in the religious ideal of a lifelong commitment between husband and wife. There was also the unquestioned assumption that stable family life was necessary for society to flourish. This sentiment was expressed by the president of Yale University in 1818 when he said, "It is incomparably better that individuals should suffer, than that an institution (marriage) that is the basis of all human good, should be shaken or endangered" (Gettleman and Markowitz, 1974: 171).

As in all societies, some early American marriages were less successful than others, and in a few cases, the local courts in the Colonial era sanctioned divorce. Divorce, however, was viewed as a measure of last resort and as a means of punishing the guilty party. Acceptable grounds were limited to desertion (for a period of no less than seven years), adultery, and impotence. Incompatibility was recognized as a serious problem but not as sufficient grounds for divorce. "Legal records reveal a variety of domestic troubles in pungent detail, e.g., a man punished for abusing his wife by kicking her off from the stool into the fire" (Demos, 1975: 12). Colonial marriages did not ordinarily end in divorce but often were dissolved by simple, but legally unrecognized, desertion; the desertion then became a grounds for divorce, if desired.

During the Colonial era, the strict matrimonial practices brought from England were gradually modified and even Puritan settlements were known to relax strict prohibitions against divorce. Legal separations and annulments became common, even when divorce was rare. It also became a commonly accepted legal practice to allow spouses to perjure themselves to obtain a divorce in jurisdictions that had restrictive grounds for divorce (Gettleman and Markowitz, 1974). The number of divorces was probably fairly high toward the end of the Colonial era, at least in the northern colonies (Rheinstein, 1972).

In the eighteenth century, as individuals began asserting greater control over their lives, there was a substantial increase in divorce. For the first time since the days of divorce laws in Ancient Rome, ordinary citizens began to consider it legitimate to leave marriages in which they were unhappy (Scanzoni, 1979).

In the nineteenth century, while there was still much guilt and shame associated with divorce, it was increasingly permitted, and in some places even encouraged. Certain states and districts where marriages could be easily dissolved became virtual divorce colonies for areas that still had restrictive provisions for divorce. State laws thus became ineffective barriers to those spouses determined to legally end their marital relationship (Gettleman and Markowitz, 1974). Divorce came to be viewed as compatible with the development of the emerging conjugal family of industrial America. The conjugal family, with weakened kin ties and control of young people, was viewed as more suitable to an industrialized economy (Goode, 1963). Individual rights and aspirations began to challenge traditional familism. Women's growing independence as a result of feminist ideals and employment outside the home significantly contributed to the continued rise in the divorce rate throughout the nineteenth century (Scanzoni, 1979). Women no longer believed they had to endure an unsatisfactory, if not oppressive, marital relationship.

In a recent analysis of historical data on divorce, Cherlin (1981) concludes that the high divorce rates today are merely a continuation of a relatively steady trend that began in the mid-nineteenth century. This study is of particular interest because of the comparison of divorce rates of the 1950s with those of the 1970s. The decade of the 1950s is often nostalgically described as representative of all that is considered "good" about family living and the prototype of family life in the first half of the twentieth century. Cherlin notes that instead of comparing today's divorce rates with divorce rates over the past 100 years, many observers err by comparing the annual rates of the 1950s, which was a time of relatively low divorce rates, with the 1970s, which was a decade of relatively high rates. "The result is to make the recent rise loom larger than it would if we took the long-term view" (p. 23). Those who married in the decade or so following World War II were the only cohorts in the last hundred years to evidence a substantial decline in the lifetime levels of divorce (see Figure 1.1). This decline in the divorce rate is often attributed to the high value placed on family life in the 1950s as a reaction to the instability of the Great Depression and World War II. The divorce rates significantly rose again in the 1970s in response to the continuation of such social changes as greater participation of women in the labor force, increased alternatives to traditional marriage, the declining stigma attached to divorce, and the rising standard for individual happiness in marriage (Cherlin, 1981; Weitzman, 1981). Cherlin's analysis thus demonstrates that the divorce rates have actually risen in a "regular fashion" since the mid-nineteenth century—the decades of the 1950s and 1970s being slight deviations.

MEASUREMENT OF DIVORCE RATES

Statistics on the frequency of divorce became available about a century ago. Until then, divorce was a rare phenomenon and was not considered important enough to warrant the collection of nationwide statistics. Starting in the mid-nineteenth century, several methods have been used to assess divorce rates. The measures most common today include the *divorce-marriage ratio, crude divorce rate, refined divorce rate, age-specific divorce rate,* and *standardized divorce rate.* However, several of these measures have serious weaknesses. They are

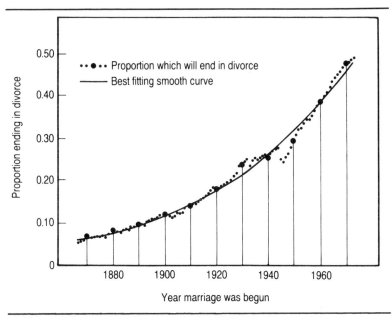

Figure 1.1: Proportion of Marriages Begun Each Year That Will End in Divorce, 1867-1973
SOURCE: Cherlin (1981). Reprinted by permission.

often insensitive to certain types of situations and trends, and thus are misleading.

The most frequently cited measure, especially in the mass media, is the *divorce-marriage ratio*, the ratio of divorces to marriages in a given year. For example, if in any given year there were 1,000 divorces and 3,000 marriages in a city, the ratio would be one divorce for every three marriages. The divorce-marriage ratio is often incorrectly interpreted; for example, it is often said today that one out of every two marriages will end in divorce or that the divorce rate is 50%, yet this is misleading. First, the divorces in the ratio are the result of marriages that began over a long time period—not the result of marriages that began in any one specific year. Yet the marriages referred to in the divorce-marriage ratio are those initiated in any one specific year. Thus, if the marriage rate dramatically increases or decreases in a given year, the divorce rate will reflect a decline or rise based largely on change in the marriage rate. If a city had only 1,000 marriages in a given year and continued to have 1,000 divorces each year, using this method of analysis, one would erroneously conclude that 100% of the marriages would end in divorce. A second reason the ratio is misleading is that approximately 20% of all marriages in a given year are remarriages; these are not analyzed separately by this measure. Thus persons who divorce and remarry in the same year would contribute to both the number of marriages and the number of divorces, again producing a divorce ratio of one divorce for each marriage or a divorce rate of 100% for this subgroup.

Another common measure of the divorce rate, often used by demographers, is the *crude divorce rate*. This is the ratio of the number of divorces to each 1,000 persons within the population in any given time span. This rate has the advantage of being easy to compute, but it has the disadvantage of using all persons as a base upon which to calculate divorce. Using all persons as a base tends to deflate the actual rate of divorce because many individuals not at risk for divorce—for example, children and unmarried adults—are included in the population base. Another disadvantage is that this crude divorce rate is influenced by the birthrate; the greater the increase in the birthrate in a given year, the lower the percentage of divorce and vice versa.

A third measure of the divorce rate is the *refined divorce rate*. It avoids the basic limitation of the crude divorce rate by comparing the number of divorces each year to the number of married women aged 15 and over—those persons who could actually be at risk for divorce. Until recently, this was the most widely accepted divorce statistic among social scientists. A major problem with the refined divorce rate is that it does not consider age differences. Younger married women tend to have substantially higher divorce rates than older married women; thus younger populations consistently have higher divorce rates than older populations. For example, the high divorce rates of recent years is highly related to the fact that the large "baby boom" generation has been passing through young adulthood.

Two other measures of divorce rates have become increasingly common: *age-specific divorce rates* and *standardized divorce rates*. Age-specific divorce rates refer to the number of divorces per 1,000 married women in various age categories. For example, one might say that a community had 37.45 divorces per 1,000 married women between the ages of 25 and 29. The major advantage of the age-specific rate is that populations with different age distributions can be compared. A disadvantage is that this measure does not yield a single summary statistic for comparison purposes (England and Kunz, 1975).

The standardized divorce rate compensates for the major weakness of the age-specific rate. The standardized divorce rate yields a single summary statistic for each population unit based on its age-specific divorce rate. The age-specific divorce rates of each population unit of interest and the corresponding frequencies in the assumed population are used to determine the expected number of divorces in each age category. The expected number of divorces is then summed across all age categories. The total is then divided by the standard population size and the result multiplied by 1,000 (Crosby, 1980). For example, the standardized divorce rate for the community above, which has an age-specific divorce rate of 37.45 divorces per 1,000 married women between the ages of 25 and 29, is 21.25—somewhat less than the rate for the 25 to 29 age group. This measure is useful because it provides a single statistic that considers age-specific variations, yet a considerable amount of specific information is lost (England and Kunz, 1975).

In addition to the weaknesses associated with the various ways the divorce rates are computed, there are serious weaknesses in the quality of the data used in these measures. National data are based only on estimates from 29 states that choose to report their divorce statistics to the National Vital Statistics Division, and these states differ in what information they report about divorce. For example, some reporting states do not report race or the number of previous marriages.

VARIATIONS IN DIVORCE RATES

As previously noted, the age of marriage typically accounts for much variation in the divorce rate. However, this is only one factor that influences the rate of divorce. Divorce rates are also affected by other factors, such as political and economic conditions, geographic differences, and various demographic characteristics. Generalizations regarding variations in divorce rates need to take into account these influences.

Societal and Economic Conditions

Societal turmoil, particularly war, is predictive of dramatic increases in divorce rates. This phenomenon was evident during the American Civil War. There were 7,380 divorces in 1860, 10,090 in 1865, and a post-war peak of 11,530 in 1866. A similar pattern has been found for World War I, World War II, the Korean War, and the Vietnam War. Several explanations have been offered to account for these wartime variations. During a war, many individuals marry after only brief courtships and thus are more likely to divorce. Other divorces are the consequences of long wartime separations and opportunities for extramarital involvement. For practical as well as patriotic reasons, relatively few individuals file for divorce while a war is in progress. However, many file after a war ends, when they find that marital readjustment cannot be achieved (Hill, 1949; Leslie, 1982).

The high divorce rate following World War II was partially attributed to the changing roles of women, that is, large numbers of women assumed occupational roles as part of the defense industry. As a result of their occupational involvement, women became more independent and assertive, and their incomes and job skills afforded them the opportunity of independent living or leaving an unsatisfactory marital relationship.

Economic conditions also influence divorce rates. Divorce, like marriage, closely follows economic cycles: low in periods of recession and depression and high during periods of prosperity. A major reason for the low divorce rate during periods of lowered economic activity is the costs involved. In addition to the costs of obtaining a divorce, costs are incurred in establishing and maintaining separate households, division of property, and providing financial support for children. These economic demands strain most people's financial resources in times of prosperity and thus divorce may become prohibitive when resources are limited. The rise in the divorce rate with economic upswings is explained by the fact that many individuals merely postpone divorce until they can afford the economic demands placed on the family's resources by divorce.

Geographic Variations

Divorce rates tend to vary by rural-urban residence and geographical region of the country. Census figures indicate divorce rates are higher in urban areas. This long-standing trend reflects the fact that divorce rates are lower in culturally homogeneous communities with face-to-face interaction, such as the rural United States. In contrast, heterogeneous communities with anonymous and/or segmentalized relationships, such as many urban areas in the United States, experience higher divorce rates (Eshleman, 1985). Primary communities, such as rural areas, are able to exert stronger formal and informal restraints on "deviant" behaviors such as divorce. Heterogeneous communities, as represented by urban areas, exert far less control over the lives of individuals. These areas thus facilitate women in obtaining jobs and achieving greater economic independence, thereby providing them more of an opportunity to leave unsatisfactory marriages (Nye and Berardo, 1973). Differences in rural-urban divorce rates also reflect a tendency for individuals from rural areas to migrate to urban areas before, during, or after a divorce. Migration occurs because urban areas offer more social and economic opportunities (Glenn and Shelton, 1985).

Divorce rates also vary by region of the country; divorce rates are the lowest in the Northeast, followed by the Midwest, the South, and, finally, the West. Explanations for these regional variations include differences in attitudes and values in the more rapidly growing sections of the country—the South and the West. The growing West and South (the "Sunbelt") conform less to tradition because they have fewer multigenerational kin and friendship groupings; these areas thus have fewer ties to the restraints of a home community, compared to the Northeast and Midwest (Fenelon, 1971). The migration to rapidly growing parts of the country may also be selective of certain personality types unusually prone to marital difficulties or characteristic of persons whose marriages are in trouble (Glenn and Shelton, 1985). These regions also tend to have younger populations, which, as previously mentioned, are more prone to divorce. Also, Blacks, who have a relatively high rate of divorce, are concentrated in the South. Another reason for regional variations in divorce rates is that the western and southern regions have higher marriage rates than other regions of the nation, thereby raising the probability that these areas will also have higher divorce rates. Finally, the religious composition of the northern and eastern regions plays an important role. Roman Catholic and Jewish populations, which have relatively low divorce rates, are overrepresented in the northern and eastern sections of the country (Glenn and Suspanic, 1984).

DEMOGRAPHIC CHARACTERISTICS

Demographic parameters are used to more precisely interpret and describe divorce rates. The *age of the spouses at the time of first marriage* is highly related to divorce. Men and women who are under the age of 20 when they first marry are two to three times more likely to divorce than their counterparts who first marry in their 20s (Alan Guttmacher Institute, 1981; Norton and Moorman, 1987). These younger individuals are typically more emotionally immature and less able to assume marital responsibilities. Those who marry at early ages are more likely to (a) be disproportionately lower class, (b) be motivated by premarital pregnancy, (c) rush into marriage for dubious reasons, such as escaping an unhappy family life, and (d) marry individuals from lower social classes (Furstenberg, 1976; Glenn and Suspanic, 1984).

Some suggest that those marrying over age 30 also have higher divorce rates than those who marry in their 20s. Individuals who delay marriage may develop an independent lifestyle that conflicts with marital role demands; women who delay marriage may establish careers with adequate incomes to maintain their desired lifestyles (Raschke, 1987). Yet some recent evidence suggests that the inverse relationship between age at first marriage and divorce is maintained after age 30 (Norton and Moorman, 1987).

Another important demographic variation is the *duration of the first marriage*. Approximately 38% of all divorces have occurred within four years of marriage, and 64% of all divorces have occurred within nine years of marriage (National Center for Health Statistics, 1986). It should be noted that the actual breakdown of the marriage usually begins well before the divorce. Many marriages that terminate in the third or fourth year of marriage may actually represent separations that occurred in the first or second year of marriage. Feelings of commitment and obligation are less likely to develop over shorter periods of time. Interestingly, there is an increasing number of couples who are divorcing after 20 or more years of marriage. In fact, the incidence of divorce for couples married 20 years or more has almost doubled in the last 20 years (Block et al., 1980). (This increase parallels the overall increase in the American divorce rate during this period.)

There is research evidence to support an inverse relation between divorce and *socioeconomic status* (e.g., Cutright, 1971; Scanzoni, 1975); higher rates of divorce exist in lower socioeconomic groups, and rates consistently decline as one moves up in socioeconomic status. Generally, this relationship has been interpreted to mean that lower socioeconomic status marriages suffer more stress and have more personal and financial problems contributing to marital instability. However, the relationship between income and divorce has been questioned. Does low income cause divorce or does divorce cause low income (Price-Bonham and Balswick, 1980)?

Also, some have found that a history of unemployment and financial instability may be more predictive of divorce than social class per se (Ross and Sawhill, 1975). Data from the 1960 and 1970 censuses and the 1975 Marital History Survey suggest that differences in divorce rates by socioeconomic status are probably decreasing (Leslie and Leslie, 1980). Thus the substantial increases in the divorce rates over the last two decades represent more of an increase among upper socioeconomic groups than lower socioeconomic groups.

In spite of very crude data, divorce rates do appear to vary by *race*. Specifically, national data indicate that the incidence of divorce is uniformly higher for Blacks than Whites. Blacks had a crude divorce rate about twice as high as Whites in 1982 (U.S. Bureau of the Census, 1983a). Although Blacks have had substantially higher divorce rates in recent years, it should be noted that the proportional increase in divorce rates for Blacks and Whites was about the same over the last two decades (U.S. Bureau of the Census, 1983a). Also, Blacks are often concentrated among lower socioeconomic groups, which are more prone to divorce. This is particularly relevant, as racial differences in divorce rates within the same income level are almost negligible (Cutright, 1971).

Divorce rates also vary by *religious affiliation*. Catholics have lower divorce rates than Protestants, but more Catholic couples are separated (Glenn and Suspanic, 1984). Differences in divorce rates have also been found among Protestant denominations; for example, conservative and fundamentalist denominations have higher divorce rates than more

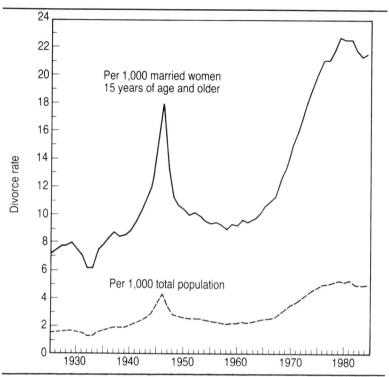

Figure 1.2: Refined Divorce Rates, United States, 1925-1984
SOURCE: National Center for Health Statistics (1986).

mainstream denominations (Raschke, 1987). In addition, religiosity, the frequency of church attendance or communion, is related to divorce; less religious individuals are more likely to divorce (Teachman, 1983).

PRESENT DIVORCE RATES

In conclusion, based on the figures and trends presented, what can be said about the present divorce rate in the United States? First, by any account, the incidence of divorce has more than doubled since the mid-1960s. Yet, in recent years there has been a significant stabilization in this trend (see Figure 1.2). The refined divorce rate in 1984 was 21.5 per 1,000 married women 15 years of age and older, only slightly more than the 1983 rate of 21.3. However, the refined divorce rate in 1979 was 22.8 and in 1980 and 1981 was 22.6 (National Center for Health Statistics, 1986).

There are two major factors that help explain this recent stabilization of divorce rates (Adams, 1986). The post-Vietnam War era of the early 1970s, like other postwar periods, was associated with unusually high divorce rates. Therefore, some stabilization would normally be expected. Second, the "baby boom" cohort (born 1946 through 1960) passed through their 20s during the decade 1965-1975—a period when this cohort of individuals would be most prone to marry and divorce. "Thus it is possible that a part of the rise from 1965-1975 was simply a function of the age of our population, and that the leveling off is in fact an indication of a high, but fairly constant, [divorce] rate in the future" (Adams, 1986: 332).

SUMMARY

Contrary to many media reports and doomsayers, one is by no means justified in concluding that a majority of all marriages today will end in divorce or even that there is an increasing incidence of divorce. Also, one cannot realistically equate divorce rates with familial or societal decay. In this chapter, evidence has been presented to suggest that some form of marital dissolution has existed throughout history and has functionally served to terminate troubled marriages. Present high rates are part of a trend extending back over 100 years as the institution of marriage adapted to the forces of industrialization and urbanization. Divorce as a social problem appears to be much greater among some sociodemographic groups than others. Yet increases over the last two decades have been very similar among all groups.

REVIEW QUESTIONS

1. Identify the major measures of divorce rates. How is each computed?
2. Why do many individuals view divorce rates with alarm?
3. Why is divorce sometimes referred to as a societal "escape valve?"
4. Compare United States divorce rates with those of other cultures, past and present.
5. Throughout the history of the United States, what factors appear to account for the consistent increase in the divorce rate?
6. What demographic factors influence divorce rates? Explain the impact of each.

SUGGESTED PROJECTS

1. Using three measures of divorce rates, determine the divorce rate of your hometown. Compare and contrast the advantages and disadvantages of the three measures.
2. Choose one highly industrialized, urbanized nation and trace its divorce rate over the twentieth century. Compare and contrast this nation's rates with those of the United States. What factors appear to account for any differences?
3. Identify a divorced individual from the media. What societal, economic, geographic, and demographic factors help to account for this person's marital status?

CHAPTER

2

Why People Divorce

There comes a time in many marriages when the couple ask a question about their relationship, a question that strikes at the roots of their lives: "Is my marriage what I need, what I dreamed of having, what I am willing to accept for the remainder of my life?" [Bernard and Hackney, 1983]

HISTORICALLY, IT HAS BEEN ASSUMED that marital happiness leads to stability while unhappiness leads to instability (Hicks and Platt, 1970). Research, however, has indicated that while marital happiness is highly related to marital stability, low marital quality does not necessarily signify a high propensity to divorce, permanently separate, or desert (Landis, 1963; Spanier and Lewis, 1980). For example, marriages are not necessarily stable merely because spouses are happy in their marriage. Rather, stable marriages may range from those that are deeply fulfilling to those characterized by feelings of entrapment, bitterness, and an atmosphere of hatred and despair (Albrecht and Kunz, 1980; Cuber and Harroff, 1965; Spanier and Thompson, 1984). Therefore, factors other than marital happiness can contribute to the stability or instability of marriages.

COST/BENEFIT ANALYSIS OF MARRIAGE

Numerous attempts have been made to determine why some couples remain married while others get divorced. Two theoretical approaches utilized to explain this dilemma are the *social exchange theory* and the *economic model*. These models both propose that individuals compare the advantages and disadvantages of their current marriages with other available alternatives, for example, another marriage or being single. As a result of this comparison, they decide whether or not to divorce.

According to the *social exchange theory,* if a relationship is rewarding, the result is an accumulation of positive sentiments, and the relationship will grow (Thibaut and Kelley, 1959). However, if the costs of the marriage are greater than the rewards, the relationship will develop more slowly and may eventually terminate. Therefore, it is

> reasonable to assume that the forecasts of future costs, as well as the memory of cumulative rewards and costs throughout the marital relationship, do generally affect both the quality and the continuance of the marital relationship. [Lewis and Spanier, 1979: 285]

The *economic model,* similar to the social exchange theory, deals directly with the costs and benefits of the current marriage versus the costs and benefits of available alternatives (Becker, 1981). Individuals compare the costs and rewards of their present relationship and determine the degree of profit (outcome a person gets as a result of remaining in the relationship). This profit is the standard used to measure the attractiveness of the relationship. If individuals view the rewards of their marriage to be at or above their costs, they will not initiate or be interested in divorce.

In spite of apparent inequities in costs and rewards, a marriage may still be acceptable if spouses can draw on other resources (Becker, 1974; Wright, 1985). These resources may include education, income, and property, as well as self-esteem, prestige, friends, and autonomy (Scanzoni and Szinovacz, 1980). The greater the number and value of these resources outside the marriage, however, the easier it is to leave an unsatisfactory relationship and secure greater rewards for less costs.

MARITAL COHESIVENESS

A detailed application of social exchange theory to divorce was presented by Levinger (1965, 1979a). According to this model, relationships have sources of attraction (positive forces that keep people in a relationship), barriers (forces that keep people from leaving a relationship), and alternative attractions (forces that compete with the attractiveness of the marital relationship).

Attractions

Attractions to the marriage include the relationship between the spouses, desire for companionship, esteem for spouse, sexual pleasure, and other affectionate aspects of the relationship. External factors, such as standard of living (home ownership and family income), high educational status, and similarity in social status also function as attractions to marriage.

Marital quality. There is much evidence to indicate marital happiness is strongly related to marital stability (Booth et al., 1983; Green and Sporakowski, 1983; Lewis and Spanier, 1979). In marriages of high quality, spouses hold intense feelings for each other, depend on each other both physically and psychologically, and hold the relationship in a preeminent position when compared to other facets of life (Cuber and Harroff, 1965).

Companionship. Some cultures do not stress the companionship role in marriage. However, most industrialized nations, faced with the decline of extended family ties, stress the importance of companionship in marriage (Goode, 1963). While many aspects of shared activities and companionship occur in the private spheres of a couple's relationship, others are scattered throughout their daily lives. Companionship repeatedly has been found to be related to marital stability as well as to marital quality (Blood and Wolfe, 1960; Levinger, 1965; Lewis and Spanier, 1979).

Esteem for spouse. The more positive the regard between spouses, the higher the marital quality (Lewis and Spanier, 1979). Spouses in happy marriages more often indicate positive evaluations of one another and describe their partners' traits as superior or equal to their own than do divorced persons (Locke, 1951; Luckey, 1964; Murstein and Glaudin, 1968). The reverse is also true; divorced women and divorce applicants report more complaints about their spouses than do spouses who report their marriages to be satisfactory (Goode, 1956; Locke, 1951).

Sexual pleasure. Most happily married couples agree that marital success does not depend on a good sexual relationship, but most also agree that a good sexual relationship contributes to their marital happiness (Strong et al., 1981). In general, couples who report greater sexual satisfaction indicate their marriage is of higher quality than couples who report low sexual satisfaction. In addition, happily married couples enjoy and desire sex significantly more often than divorced persons (Locke, 1951).

The source of sexual satisfaction may differ for men and women (Nye and Berardo, 1973). Burgess and Wallin (1953) found that dissatisfaction with sexual intercourse predicted dissatisfaction with the marriage for husbands but not for wives. The relationship between sex and marital happiness appears to be more complicated for women because of their emphasis on intimacy (Leslie, 1982). Also, women who rate their marriages as very good or good have reported they have orgasms all or most of the time (Bell, 1979).

Income. Since the early part of this century, the divorce rate has, in general, been negatively associated with the husband's income. Lower income individuals have a greater propensity for divorce than those in higher income groups (see Chapter 1). It appears that for those with lower incomes, the attractions of marriage are low while the attractions outside marriage are high. For example, both White and Black men, ages 45 to 54 years who "had everything going for them" with regard to education, occupation, and earnings were more likely to be married in 1970 than men who "had very little going for them" (Carter and Glick, 1976).

It may not be the amount of income per se that is related to the propensity to divorce. Rather, it may be other factors, including a person's expectations and attitudes toward income (Coombs and Zumeta, 1970), the difference between actual and expected income (Becker et al., 1977), or the stability of earnings (Ross and Sawhill, 1975). In addition, the positive relation between income and marital stability may be indirect. Personal factors that are common to success in both marriage and occupation produce greater economic resources that, in turn, result in the reduction of some of the factors that contribute to interpersonal tension (crowding, disagreeable living conditions, competition for a limited amount of money) (Ross and Sawhill, 1975). In addition, higher incomes afford a couple a potentially more satisfactory level of consumption, resulting in both spouses maintaining a more positive view of their lifestyle. Such situations contribute to higher levels of mutual affect between husbands and wives.

Home ownership. Owning monetary assets and, in particular, owning a home, are associated with a lower likelihood of getting a divorce (Galligan and Bahr, 1978; South and Spitz, 1986). Home ownership can indicate the degree of investment a couple has in their marriage (South and Spitze, 1986). Homeowners are also less likely to dissolve their marriage because of the detrimental effects it might have on their investment.

Level of education. Higher levels of education are generally associated with more stable marriages (Becker et al., 1977; Coombs and Zumeta, 1970; Mott and Moore, 1979; South and Spitze, 1986). Recent findings indicate that the highest marital disruption rates exist for males and females who did not graduate from high school. This is not to imply that divorce is rare among highly educated persons, because a sharp increase in the proportion of separated and divorced has occurred at all educational levels (Carter and Glick, 1976). In addition, persons who start college but do not finish have a higher rate of divorce than persons who complete high school but do not pursue a college degree. This phenomenon has been attributed to those individuals' having personality traits or social characteristics that decrease their general persistence level (Thornton, 1978).

Similar social status. There have been numerous studies that indicate spouses having homogamous social characteristics, such as race, religion, education, and age, experience higher marital quality than spouses with hetergamous characteristics (Lewis and Spanier, 1979). Research on the divorce rates of interracial marriages have yielded conflicting findings—perhaps indicating it might be premature to conclude that differences in race are related to marital instability (Burr, 1976). Some research has indicated Black-White marriages (Carter and Glick, 1976) and Oriental-White marriages (Miller, 1971) have a greater probability of divorce. In contrast, a review of divorce records in Iowa over a 30-year period indicated Black-White marriages were more stable than Black-Black or White-White marriages (Monahan, 1970). Currently, interracial marriages more often occur between persons who are economically and educationally equal and who have a strong emotional attachment (Eshleman, 1985). Consequently, even though mixed-race marriages may experience negative external pressures, these pressures may help to solidify or stabilize these marriages (Burr, 1976; Cheng and Yamamura, 1957; Kimura, 1957; Monahan, 1970; Smith, 1966).

The research findings on the relation between interfaith marriage and marital dissolution are not consistent. Jewish-Gentile marriages have been found to have higher divorce rates than Jewish-Jewish marriages, yet Jewish-Gentile marriages are often characterized by childlessness or a small number of children, or involve previously married individuals (Moller, 1975). Protestant-Catholic marriages also have a higher divorce rate than religiously homogamous marriages; however, the Catholic spouse is more often religiously inactive prior to marriage (Bumpass and Sweet, 1972). This relation, however, is confounded by the fact that persons who marry outside their faith, compared to persons who marry within their faith, are more likely to have been previously married, to have had a civil rather than a religious marriage ceremony, to have parents who were involved in a mixed-religion marriage, to have a high rate of premarital pregnancy, and to have an urban background—all factors that have been found to be related to higher rates of dissolution (Kephart, 1981).

Since 1960, the educational level of husbands and wives has moved sharply upward. "As a consequence, more and more college educated persons now can—and, in fact, do—marry persons with a similar amount of education" (Carter and Glick, 1976: 411-412). This similarity in educational levels has been found to be positively related to marital quality (Lewis and Spanier, 1979). In contrast, there are higher rates of marital instability for (a) couples in which the wife had not completed high school and the husband has attended college, (b) wives who graduated from high school married to men who graduated from college, and (c) college-educated women who married high school dropouts (Bumpass and Sweet, 1972).

People in American society tend to marry others within their own age group (Strong and DeVault, 1986). Available data show the difference in median age of husbands and wives is approximately 2½ years (Eshleman, 1985). This similarity in the ages is positively related to marital satisfaction (Blood and Wolfe, 1960; Burgess and Cottrell, 1939). This relation has been attributed to people viewing themselves as members of a generation, with their consequent experience of life resulting in different values and expectations. Furthermore, different developmental and life tasks (parenting, earning capacity, retirement) confront us at different ages. By marrying people of similar ages, the congruence of developmental tasks is ensured (Strong and DeVault, 1986).

Barriers

Barriers to leaving a marriage include feelings of obligation and external pressures to stay married. These may include dependent children, feelings of loyalty to the marital bond, moral proscriptions associated with religion and church attendance, external pressures such as families and community stigma, and legal and economic barriers.

Religion. Religion as a barrier to divorce may be weakening in our society. However, it has historically functioned as a strong barrier to divorce. While no religion advocates divorce, the Catholic Church has the most formalized sanctions against it. Not surprisingly, Catholics have a lower rate of marital dissolution than Protestants (Coombs and Zumeta, 1970; Thornton, 1978) (see Chapter 1). However, this trend may be changing; divorce among practicing Catholics was a major ingredient in the accelerated divorce rates of the 1960s and 1970s. By the latter decade, 1960s Catholics had become assimilated into the mainstream of American life, that is, there was a lessening of dependence on doctrine or dogma for personal direction. Their divorce rate reflected this assimilation. However, compared with other religious groups, Catholic couples who separate are less likely to obtain a divorce. Therefore, the Catholic religion appears to inhibit divorce, but does not seem to inhibit separation (Young, 1978).

Many assume a high positive correlation between low divorce rates and membership in fundamentalist religions. This does not appear to be true. Fundamentalist and Baptist women have been reported to have higher dissolution rates than Catholics or other women (Thornton, 1978). The rationale behind these higher divorce rates has been attributed to inflexibility and rigidity of position, a focus on the next life rather than the current one, or to the generally lower socioeconomic status of these groups (Eshleman, 1985).

Children. Children have been viewed as a barrier to marital dissolution, but there are indications this barrier also may be weakening. Thornton found a decrease over time in those believing that "when there are children in the family, parents should stay together, even if they don't get along" (Thornton, 1985: 871). Having a baby, however, does appear to decrease marital dissolution for the child's first two years (Waite et al., 1985). This is attributed to the expense of children in time, money, and effort during this time. In addition, preschool-age children are viewed as representing a significant cost for a woman if she separates from her husband and retains custody of the children (Mott and Moore, 1979).

The presence of preschool-age children may also be a barrier to divorce for men who fear being separated from their young children. In contrast, women may contemplate ending a marriage and gaining independence only when children are old enough for single parenthood to be feasible (Huber and Spitze, 1980; South and Spitze, 1986). Therefore, while marital satisfaction is lower when children are younger, the barriers to dissolution are greater.

Childless couples appear to have substantially higher divorce rates than couples with children (Bumpass and Sweet, 1972). However, this relationship is very complex because it is unclear whether childlessness is the result of marital disruption or the higher rate of divorce is due to childlessness.

Legal and economic barriers. The structure of divorce laws and procedures has changed radically in recent years (Freed and Walker, 1986). Liberalization of divorce laws, through the creation of "no-fault" divorce, has resulted in a reduction in the legal barriers to divorce. Evidence indicates that divorce rates are higher in states where "no-fault" divorce laws exist (Stetson and Wright, 1975; Wright and Stetson, 1978). The removal of this legal barrier may have more effect on men than women because the proportion of the sexes initiating and completing divorce procedures has reversed (Gunter, 1977) (see Chapter 6).

Family income. Families with higher incomes are better able to divide their resources and support two households than are families with lower incomes. However, recent media coverage regarding fathers' failure to comply with child support awards may result in distrust on the part of women, therefore resulting in a strong emerging barrier to divorce. Likewise, for women with lower levels of education and a lack of job skills, marriage may be their only alternative because of their disadvantage in the labor force.

Higher-income couples can also experience economic constraints against separation and divorce. A couple's money may be invested in nonliquid assets, preventing their division, or if a couple's assets were to be divided, each might experience a lower level of consumption (Coombs and Zumeta, 1970). Consequently, even higher-income couples may find money a barrier to divorce.

Obligations to the marital bond. While divorced persons who remarry are more likely to remain married until the death of one spouse than they are to divorce (Glick and Norton, 1977), there are indications that they may be more likely to consider a divorce because some barriers to divorce have already been weakened. In general, research findings indicate that for people previously divorced, marital dissolution is higher in second marriages and higher still in third marriages (Bumpass and Sweet, 1972; Glick and Norton, 1977). In addition, the median length of each succeeding marriage that ends in divorce is shorter than previous marriages (Eshleman, 1985).

The number of years a person has invested in a marriage also acts as a barrier to divorce. This is evident in that the largest number of divorce decrees are granted one to three years after marriage, with the number consistently declining with increased duration (Eshleman, 1985).

Community stigma. Community disapproval also serves as a barrier to marital dissolution. There are indications marital stability is related to (a) the more friends members of a couple have in common and as individuals, (b) the more embedded a couple is in the community, and (c) the more voluntary organizations a couple is active in (Lewis and Spanier, 1979). This visibility can result in greater restraints on spouses against social transgressions that could lead to divorce (Blood, 1962) as well as against consideration of divorce. This visibility is greater in rural areas where there are more primary relationships and where the social network is more tightly organized than in urban or suburban areas. Therefore, rural couples experience greater restraints, resulting in lower divorce rates, as noted in Chapter 1.

Family influence. Children's marriages are more susceptible to divorce if their parents were divorced. This phenomena has been attributed to various reasons, including personality characteristics, reduction in economic resources, attitudes of permissiveness, lack of social control, and lack of opportunity for children to learn appropriate behavior for marital roles (Pope and Mueller, 1979).

Parents who do not divorce may serve as a barrier to their children divorcing. For example, parents and other family members may socialize their children to view divorce as an inappropriate response to marital difficulties. In addition, intact families may provide more social control over a child than single-parent families because they are more likely to discipline a child for bad behavior, control peer contacts, influence the choice of a mate, and support a contracted marriage. In addition, because the size and integration of a child's kin network is greater for intact families, its effectiveness as a social control mechanism may also be greater than for divorced families (Mueller and Pope, 1977). Marital quality in the family of orientation is also positively associated with marital quality in families of procreation. Similarly, the more positive a relationship is between parents and children, and the greater the support from parents, friends, and in-laws, the better the children's marital quality and the less likely they are to divorce (Lewis and Spanier, 1979).

Alternatives

Circumstances that afford an alternative to marriage include the availability of resources outside the marriage, higher levels of education (particularly for women), employment opportunities, the desirability of being single, and alternative sources of affection.

Economic resources. Income Maintenance Programs may offer an economic alternative to an unsatisfactory marriage. These programs have been proposed as a means to reduce divorce rates. The assumption underlying these programs is that if income among lower-class families is increased, marital instability will be more costly, thus divorce rates will decline. However, the opposite appears to occur. In Denver, Colorado, and Seattle, Washington, large increases in marital instability occurred after an Income Maintenance Program was implemented (Cutright, 1971; Hannan et al., 1978).

> Our findings imply that, if the entire sample were enrolled in an income-maintenance program with a low support level, the annual probability of marital dissolution would increase 63% for Blacks, 194% for Whites, and 83% for Chicanos over what it would be in a control situation. [Hannan et al., 1978: 1206]

In contrast, the impact of programs such as AFDC on divorce rates is unclear. Scanzoni (1975) concluded welfare payments did not contribute to divorce. However, Honig (1973) concluded that, other things being equal, if the AFDC stipend increases 10%, the proportion of female family heads may increase by 20% for Whites and 14% for non-Whites. It is not clear, however, if these increases in the rates of female-headed households are the result of higher separation rates or lowered remarriage rates. It could mean that the availability of welfare payments or Income Maintenance Programs may offer an alternative to women, thereby eliminating some of the necessity of families staying together for economic reasons.

Education. In general, negative correlation exists between educational level and marital dissolution. However, the exception to this relationship is among women with five or more years of higher education (Houseknecht and Spanier, 1980; South and Spitze, 1986). This exception is attributed to the indirect effect of education on income through occupational levels, thereby affording more highly educated women more alternatives outside of marriage. Education for women also results in increased prestige and access to resources. There has also been a slight increase in marital dissolution for males with six-plus years of college. This trend, however, was attributed to the increase in more highly educated males marrying more highly educated females (Houseknecht and Spanier, 1980).

Employment opportunities. Lower earnings of women, compared to men, may contribute to lower rates of marital dissolution. In contrast, it seems logical that if women have economic resources available to them, their behavioral autonomy will be increased, thereby reducing their dependence on husbands and contributing to a higher divorce rate.

Several studies have indicated that the probability of divorce is directly related to the amount of wages earned by women (Hannan et al., 1978; Johnson, 1985; Sawhill, 1975). Conversely, marriages are more stable if the ratio of the wife's wage relative to her husband's is low (Becker, 1974), and an increase in the wife's earnings not only increases the probability of divorce but also reduces her propensity to remarry (Becker et al., 1977). These findings have been attributed to (a) the independence of women as a result of employment (Ross and Sawhill, 1975), (b) the disruptive effect created by changes in traditional work roles (Cherlin, 1981), (c) wives actually working as a form of "divorce insurance," and (d) time constraints of the wife's employment, which create conflict about the division of household labor and lower rates of spousal interaction (Spitze and South, 1985).

Economic factors that can contribute to marriage dissolution should be differentiated from those that have a positive impact on marriage (Ross and Sawhill, 1975). For example, among lower income groups in which the husband's income is low, the wife's earnings make a big difference in the family's ability to maintain its desired standard of living; therefore, wives' earnings are viewed as having a positive impact on marriage (Blood and Wolfe, 1960).

Single life. In recent years, the stigma previously associated with divorce has faded and a divorce is no longer seen as a mark of failure

(Cherlin, 1981). This change in society's attitudes has altered life after divorce for many people. Today, after-divorce alternatives include the possibility of trying new activities or resuming hobbies that may have been dropped while married. Those divorced persons who have the time, energy, and money may travel, return to school, change jobs, or seek new social relationships. Some persons view this period as a stimulating time filled with exciting new challenges (Kaslow, 1984).

Sources of affection. When assessing personal alternatives to their present marriages, many individuals take inventory of their current resources and consider what kind of life they would have if they no longer were married (Kessler, 1975). They must also make an assessment of the value of their spouses, that is, those qualities, skills, or contributions the spouses bring to the marriage. In essence, can they get someone better? (Udry, 1981). Based on social exchange theory, it is assumed that the greater a person's resources (education, income-producing capacity, attractiveness, age), the greater the likelihood the person can replace his or her spouse with one of equal or higher quality and the more likely the marriage will end.

Because of the prevailing economically dependent position of many women, the possibility of replacing a spouse is more important to them than it is to men. Therefore, the consideration of replacing a spouse might act as a barrier, rather than as an alternative, for women (Udry, 1981).

WHY PEOPLE SAY
THEY GET DIVORCED

When couples divorce, they usually do not give the previously discussed theories as reasons for the divorce. Instead, they present specific complaints regarding their marriages or their spouses. It is highly unlikely that divorced persons' provide objective descriptions of their previous marriages. Recalling the past is often painful, and accounts are a deliberate construction of "what went wrong" (Weiss, 1975). But these subjective interpretations have an importance all their own (Goode, 1956) because they represent the divorced person's struggle to "make sense" of his or her divorce. It is common for a person to fashion his or her marital complaints into "accounts—a history of the marital failure, a story of what their spouse did, what they did, and what happened in consequence" (Weiss, 1975: 14)—a process that offers some reduction of distress.

Although personal descriptions usually lack objectivity, research on divorce has provided several methodological consistencies that allow us to make some tentative conclusions (Bloom et al., 1985). For example, in 1948, Goode (1956) interviewed 425 divorced women in metropolitan Detroit. Between 29% and 33% of the respondents indicated that the primary reason(s) for their marriage ending in divorce were husband's (a) nonsupport, (b) excessive authoritarianism, (c) combinations of drinking, gambling, and infidelity, (d) excessive drinking, and (e) personality problems or personal incompatibility. Nonsupport and excessive authoritarianism were more often mentioned by women who had been married for a relatively short period of time than by those who had been married for a longer period of time. In contrast, (a) lack of interest in the home, (b) excessive drinking, (c) infidelity, and (d) the combination of drinking, gambling, and running around with other women were more often mentioned by women married for a longer period of time. Based on these data, Goode concluded that there were two basic dimensions underlying these complaints—disagreement and involvement in the home. In his study of 600 couples who had applied for divorce in Cleveland, Ohio, Levinger (1966) found social class differences in the type of legal complaints. He categorized the complaints into 11 areas. These areas included neglect of home or children, financial problems, physical abuse, mental abuse, infidelity, sexual incompatibility, drinking, in-law trouble, mental cruelty, lack of love, and excessive demands. Compared to middle-class respondents, lower-class respondents were more likely to mention failure to perform instrumental family tasks because of inadequate financial resources, excessive drinking, and physical abuse as the reasons for divorce. Middle-class respondents focused less on instrumental tasks and more on affective relationships. They complained about the lack of love, infidelity, and excessive demands. Wives had almost twice as many complaints as husbands, and wives' complaints were significantly more frequent in the following areas: physical abuse, verbal abuse, financial problems, drinking, neglect of home or children, mental cruelty, and lack of love. Only in two categories, in-law trouble and sexual incompatibility, did husbands have significantly more complaints than wives.

Kitson and Sussman (1982) investigated the marital complaints of 209 persons who had filed for divorce in Cleveland, Ohio, in the mid 1970s. Using Goode's (1956) original categorization of complaints and a supplementary scale, they found that women had more complaints than men. Furthermore, the women were more likely to focus their complaints on their spouse's personality, authoritarianism, drinking, sexual problems, non-support, and infidelity. Men more often complained about their wife's infidelity and problems with relatives. In addition, when they compared a matched subsample of their respondents with Goode's sample, they found major differences in the sources of marital dissatisfaction between the two samples. For example, complaints about personality and home life were cited most frequently in the Cleveland study but were ranked fifth and sixth in the Detroit study. Secondly, nonsupport was ranked first in 1948, but twelfth in 1975.

In addition, Kitson (1985) reported men were more likely than women to be unsure about what caused the breakup of their marriage. They were also more likely to mention overcommitment to work, problems with relatives, and external events, such as a death in the family, a job change, or involvement with a third party, as reasons for divorce. Women, in contrast, were more likely to mention that the following factors led to the breakup of their marriage: extramarital sex, untrustworthiness or immaturity, being out with the boys, drinking, financial and employment problems, and emotional and personality problems.

Thurnher et al. (1983) collected data from 199 women and 134 men in the San Francisco area. Among these respondents, the most common reasons for seeking a divorce included lifestyle conflicts, infidelity of the spouse, financial problems, and sexual difficulties. Gender differences were observed. Women were more likely to mention spouse violence, infidelity, and drinking, whereas men were more likely to mention spouse's desire for freedom.

Bloom et al. (1985) interviewed 153 persons about their sources of marital dissatisfaction. They used, with minor changes, Levinger's (1966) list of marital complaints. Respondents were asked to describe their complaints as well as what they believed their spouse's complaints were about them. The most frequently reported area of marital dissatisfaction was personal incompatibility, which included communication difficulties, value conflicts, boredom, verbal abuse, and sexual difficulties. Also, respondents reported their spouses had numerous complaints about them, and they and their spouses held similar views about their marriage and its difficulties. In addition, Bloom et al. found few significant gender differences.

Some 205 couples who had been granted or had filed for a divorce or a child support agreement in conjuction with separation in Pennsylvania were interviewed in Spanier and Thompson's (1983) study. In contrast to earlier studies, instead of asking respondents to generate the "causes" of the divorce, they asked respondents to evaluate their marriage along dimensions associated with marital stability, that is, their degree of disappointment with the spouse's performance about a range of instrumental and expressive domains, task participation at home, financial instability, and marital sex relations. Similar to Levinger (1966) and Kitson and Sussman (1982), wives were more disappointed than the husbands in most areas of partner performance. In general, where spousal expectations were expressive and shared (such as talking things over) or where the partner rated the other's performance in an area traditionally assigned to one's own gender, disappointment was typical. Wives were generally more disappointed in their husband's role performance than vice versa. These studies indicate that over time, reasons for divorcing one's spouse have changed. The reasons mentioned in Goode's study can be described as "more serious" (nonsupport, issues of authority, and activities involved in the family's social life). The reasons given in more recent studies often involve personal incompatibility and personal growth issues. This change has been attributed to our changing view of marriage. Marriage is increasingly viewed as a source of interpersonal nurturance and individual gratification (Bloom et al., 1985). Individuals are now more concerned about the emotional aspects of marriage and the provision of an emotionally healthy environment for raising children (Kitson et al., 1982). Another explanation for the change in reasons given for divorce has been attributed to a shift in the legal system away from having to demonstrate fault (Hunt and Hunt, 1977). It is also clear from these studies that men and women experience divorce differently (Albrecht, 1980; Green and Sporakowski, 1983). These differences range from the reasons for divorcing to their experiences after divorce. Women's reasons for divorce do not usually include such factors as self-actualization or fulfillment—both dominant themes in the popular literature on divorce. Rather, their reasons seem to reflect the realization that any further personal action or sacrifice will not remedy an intolerable situation (Thurnher et al., 1983). In contrast, it may be that men are more influenced than women by events, opportunities, and audiences external to their marriages in the divorce decision-making process.

SUMMARY

The basic theoretical approaches to explaining why people divorce center around exchange theory, which accounts for divorce in terms of costs and rewards. Levinger's (1965) exchange model included the concepts of attractions to marriage, barriers against divorce, and alternatives to marriage. Societal change, including the increasing acceptance of divorce, is evident in the weakening in the barriers to divorce. Few segments of our society have not experienced divorce—regardless of religious affiliation, the presence of children, income, geographical location, or family backgrounds.

Reasons people give for divorce also reflect these weakened barriers. Recently, these reasons have focused on individual welfare and personal growth. In the past, reasons for divorce reflected the family's instrumental role in the larger community.

REVIEW QUESTIONS

1. What are the major theoretical approaches used to explain why people divorce?
2. Attractions, barriers, and alternatives influence whether or not a person gets a divorce. Differentiate between these three factors. How does each act independently in determining whether or not people divorce?
3. What are the primary reasons people give for getting divorced? How have these reasons changed in the last few decades?
4. How do men and women differ in the reasons they give for getting a divorce? Why do you think this difference exists?

SUGGESTED PROJECTS

1. Interview three divorced men and three divorced women about the primary reasons they got a divorce. Compare these reasons with the research literature.
2. Identify barriers and attractions in long-standing marriages that end in divorce.
3. Compare the etiology of divorce with the etiology of a dating relationship that breaks up. What are the similarities and what are the differences?

CHAPTER

3

Separation

To free oneself is nothing; it's being free that's hard. [André Gide, 1869-1951]

DIVORCE IS A PROCESS that starts long before a final decision is reached. This process continues through the end of the marriage, the separation, legal action, and resolutions a couple must come to about their continued relationship with each other, their children, and the larger society (Wiseman, 1975).

Almost all couples experience separation at sometime during their marriage, for example, one spouse goes on a business trip or to visit relatives. However, separation, as referred to in this book, does not include these normal separations. Here, separation refers to couples who are living apart with the intention of getting a divorce or those who are permanently or temporarily separated because of marital discord (Carter and Glick, 1976).

Not all separations end in divorce. For many couples, however, it is a stage in the divorce process; the couple separates in order to file for a divorce or in order to decide if they actually want a divorce. Other couples may select separation instead of divorce. Specifically, this action ordinarily includes those persons who cannot afford a divorce and those who belong to religious groups that oppose divorce (Kitson and Raschke, 1981).

INCIDENCE AND FREQUENCY
OF SEPARATION

In spite of the view that separation is a very important period in the divorce process, there is little demographic data available. This lack of data is attributed partially to the fact that, unlike marriage and divorce, separation is more often an informal arrangement between spouses (Bloom et al., 1977; Cherlin, 1981). In some states, a period of separation is required in order to obtain a divorce, but in other states couples do not necessarily separate until the final divorce is decreed. For example, Kitson and Langlie (1984) found 27% of their sample (n = 148) did not physically separate from their spouses at any point in the divorce-filing process.

Several sources of data, including the U.S. Bureau of the Census, reveal some indication of the incidence of separation. This agency began enumerating "married persons with the spouse absent" in 1930. In 1950, they split separations into those associated with marital discord and those due to other causes, such as employment, military duty, or other legal, physical, or mental health reasons (Carter and Glick, 1976).

In 1984, the U.S. Bureau of Census reported that in 1983, 4,198,000 persons or 2.4% of the U.S. population were separated from their spouses because of marital discord. These data have been questioned because of conflicting reports. For example, in 1970, 1,317,620 women but only 873,471 men reported they were separated from their spouses. This discrepancy has been attributed to individuals, especially never-married mothers, who may hesitate admitting they are not married and the fact that women may be more willing to admit their marriages are in trouble (Cherlin, 1981; Kitson, 1985).

Some researchers, however, have reported data concerning separation. Weiss (1975), based on his Seminars for the Separated, estimated approximately one-half of all married couples separate at least once before the final separation associated with divorce. Similarly, Kitson (1985) found 42% of the divorced suburban individuals in her longitudinal study had separated and reconciled at least once before initiating a divorce.

Bloom et al. (1977) conducted an extensive telephone survey of 2,000 households in Boulder County, Colorado. They found 62 couples had separated during the previous year because of marital conflict. When they extrapolated these data to the entire population of the county, they concluded that 1,820 couples had separated during that year, or 4.6% of all couples. During the same time period, 1,123 couples, or 2.8% of the population, divorced. Therefore, the incidence of separation was far greater than the incidence of divorce. They also found, in a random sample of the same geographical area (n = 2,940), 17% of those persons who had ever been married had separated from their spouses at least once.

Multiple Separations

The frequency of multiple separations or the correlates of separation, such as race and income, are often not reported. In fact, some couples appear to engage in a repeated pattern of separation and reconciliation. For example, people in marriages characterized by alcoholism often develop a repeated pattern in which the alcoholic partner apologizes and promises to change. In response, his or her partner hopes or believes things will get better in the future and the couple reconciles, only to separate again (Dobash and Dobash, in Kitson, 1985). Kitson (1985) also conducted a survey (n = 1,039) in the Cleveland, Ohio, area and found 16% of those who had either been married, were married, or were cohabiting, were separated. Over one-half of these respondents (54.5%) reported at least two separations, and 26.7% reported four or more separations. Furthermore, persons in their second or third marriage were more likely to have separated in the past as well as in their current relationships.

Racial Differences

Using data based on the 1973 National Survey of Family Growth, Cherlin (1981) reported strong racial differences in separation. He estimated that within 10 years of their first marriage, about 40% of Black women and 20% of White women will separate (assuming the level of separation reported in 1973 continued). In 1979, 15% of all Black women, aged 25 to 44, were currently separated, as compared to 3% of all White women of the same age. However, once separated, Black women took longer to obtain a divorce than did White women; five years after their separation, about one-half of all separated Black women were still separated, compared to only about 10% of all White women.

Separations That End in Divorce

Bloom et al. (1977) reported that close to 90% of the separated couples in their study divorced. Other data, however, indicate that this high percentage is the exception because separation does not necessarily lead to the filing for divorce. Kitson (1985) found in her study that only 18.2% of those currently married who had ever separated had filed for divorce, and only about one-third who were currently separated had filed.

Separation is more prevalent than divorce because it serves functions other than ending a marriage. It can be an attempt by one or both spouses to emphasize the unhappiness of the marriage, or it may provide a period of time for spouses to decide whether or not they want to divorce. Marital separations have been found to be associated with greater marital unhappiness. However, they may be less disruptive than they appear, merely reflecting normal transitions in generally satisfying marriages (Kitson, 1985).

THE DECISION TO SEPARATE

Most separations occur after the marriage has been dysfunctional for a long period of time (Cuber and Harroff, 1965). Some couples, however, report that their marriages were generally satisfactory, and it was only during the final months before actual separation that they experienced conflict and/or began leading emotionally and behaviorally separate lives (Spanier and Thompson, 1983).

Regardless of the situation, the pre-separation period is a decision-making phase (Brown et al., 1980). Obviously, this decision is regarded as major because it has major consequences for a person's own life, as well as for others associated with that person. Therefore, it is likely to include periods of indecision (Tyiere and Peacock, 1982).

This decision-making process includes the foreboding of possible consequences of a marital breakup. Women may take a longer period of time to decide on separation. Spanier and Thompson (1983) found that women spent an average of 22 months, whereas men spent only 12 months, making the decision; the average length of time was even longer when the divorce was mutually desired.

In contrast, there are some people who experience little indecision regarding their separation. These individuals are certain about their desire to terminate their present relationship and appear to have no regrets beyond some natural sentiments. In these cases, the spouses do not experience guilt, shame, anxiety, or fear; instead, they feel like they have discarded a heavy burden.

LENGTH OF SEPARATION

The period of separation, before a final divorce or reconciliation, may vary from several weeks to several years—depending on the couple and legal procedures involved. Goode (1956), in his study of divorced women, found that 40% of the separations occurred over one-year prior to the final divorce. Monahan (1962) found a median duration of 2 to 5 years in the period between separation and divorce in Wisconsin. Similarly, Raschke and Barringer (1977) reported spouses spent an average of two years between separation and divorce, and Bloom et al. (1977) found the period of separation averaged 13.8 months. Therefore, most couples spend considerable time between separation and divorce.

The recent liberalization of divorce laws has been accompanied by a reduction in some of the legal complications that prolonged the procedure in the past. At the same time, most states have established a minimum period of separation between the filing of the petition for dissolution and the final decree. Therefore, regardless of when a person files a petition for dissolution, there is almost always, by necessity, a legally defined period of separation prior to divorce.

WHO MAKES THE DECISION

Spanier and Thompson (1983) reported almost 2/3 of the women in their study claimed to have first suggested the divorce. This is almost identical to Goode's (1956) findings. Goode speculated, however, that it is actually more often the husband who first wants to end the marriage, and he maneuvers the wife into suggesting a divorce because it is considered unmanly to suggest fault in a wife/mother. As evidence for this contention, Goode reported that the length of deliberation between serious consideration and filing for divorce is much shorter when the husband suggested the divorce. Spanier and Thompson (1983) did not substantiate this finding, and Dixon and Weitzman (1982) reported that when men file, they do so believing they will have a better chance of receiving a favorable settlement.

The process of "maneuvering" has been described by Federico (1979) as the point of "no return" for at least one partner. Through this process, the partner who initially wants the divorce engages in actions reflecting progressive dissatisfaction with, or withdrawal from, the relationship. The goal, which is to provide the other partner with a reason to declare the marriage over, is achieved through provocation. The goal may not be reached when the provoked spouse accommodates and/or sabotages the maneuvering by reacting with face-saving or relationship-balancing acts.

Female-initiated divorces may appear to be in contradiction to the long-held assumption that marriage is a more desired status for women than for men. But, when a woman takes the initiative in divorce, she is not necessarily rejecting marriage, only a husband. In fact, family roles are viewed as playing a more central role in the lives of women than of men and can result in women having less toleration for a bad marriage. In addition, men have more opportunities to become attached to other women. While they may not be seeking other attachments that can complicate their lives and perhaps lead to a divorce, these relationships do provide strong legal grounds for divorce. In fact, most grounds for divorce have traditionally been focused on male behavior (Nye and Berardo, 1973), resulting in women initiating divorce.

STAGES IN THE PROCESS

Several authors have developed models describing the various stages of divorce, including the preseparation, separation, and post-legal decree. These models can be divided into two basic categories (Salts, 1979): (a) those that focus on feelings (Froiland and Hozman, 1977; Kraus, 1979; Wiseman, 1975) and (b) those that delineate states of being that incorporate these feelings (Kessler, 1975; Waller, 1951). These models are not contradictory. Rather, they differ in the emphasis placed on events and the beginning and ending points in the divorce process. However, all models stipulate that people experience divorce differently; some skip stages, some alter the sequence of stages, and some are simultaneously in more than one stage (Salts, 1979). It is evident, according to most models, that the majority of the stages take place before the couple separates (see Price-Bonham and Balswick, 1980; Salts, 1979).

Kessler (1975) described the origin of divorce as beginning when disillusionment with the marriage or spouse first occurs. During this stage, spouses begin to realize that real differences exist in their marriage. They may continue to laugh and interact in public; however, their private life starts to suffer and there is a concentration on the negative. Attraction and trust for each other starts to wane.

> Disillusionment chips away at the enchantment process. The person who was to fulfill almost all your expectations, needs, and ideals turned out to be depressed, sloppy, a compulsive eater, uninformed, unaffectionate, asocial, domineering, insensitive, uncaring, a flirt, nagging, overly dependent, overly self-sufficient, oversexed or any other characteristic that isn't compatible with your needs. The honeymoon is over. [Kessler, 1975: 21]

If these differences are not discussed and resolved, a couple will move into the erosion stage (Kessler, 1975). Bohannan (1970) described this stage as the emotional divorce, when spouses withhold emotions from the relationship. During this stage, there is a continuation of the wearing away of marital satisfaction, and one spouse realizes the costs of staying in the marriage are greater than the rewards being received. This stage is often characterized by repressed anger and hurt being expressed, and problems such as ulcers, migraine headaches, anxiety, and impotence may emerge. The marital relationship may be characterized by dagger looks, interruptions, contradiction of one another, and fierce competition. Spouses maintain a careful vigil to make sure one does not give more than the other; they concentrate on taking rather than giving and on being loved rather than loving. While disillusionment remains in the mind, erosion invokes behaviors that have the goal of advantageously changing the perceived hierarchy between spouses.

During this stage, couples may deny that the relationship is deteriorating (Juhasy, 1979; Wiseman, 1975). In order to maintain the relationship, spouses insist they are adjusted, can work to accommodate the situation, or even prefer it the way it is. This stage may involve spouses using an external rationale, such as finances or children, to keep themselves from considering divorce. Some couples maintain this status quo for years whereas others improve their relationship or move toward divorce (Salts, 1979).

If the erosion stage is not reversed, the detachment stage follows (Kessler, 1975). This stage involves a series of emotional deaths that result in spouses no longer investing in their marriage. It is characterized by nonverbal behavior that may include eyes cast down or looking past each other, bodies turned away from each other, arms and legs locked—all designed to symbolically block out the other person. Voices may be harsh and strident or barely audible and faces may mask feelings. There is not much conflict during this stage, primarily because of boredom and lack of involvement.

During this time one or both spouses may switch from thinking about the past and present to the future—without their spouse. They may fantasize about what single life would be like, assessing the financial gains and losses of divorce as well as their appeal to the opposite sex.

This lack of interest may be experienced by only one spouse. For the other partner, the realization of disinterest may bring about such responses as bargaining (offering sexual favors or changing interaction patterns), or hoping that the one who is detached will change his/her mind (Froiland and Hozman, 1977; Juhasy, 1979).

Eventually, the end of the marriage becomes a reality, and depression may turn to anger; yet the rejected spouse often remains ambivalent about ending the marriage. However, it may become increasingly evident that neither spouse has a real interest in continuing the marital relationship (Wiseman, 1975).

Physical separation is the most traumatic aspect of the divorce process (Bohannan, 1970; Chester, 1971; Kessler, 1975; Weiss, 1975). It is a public declaration of marital discord (Chiriboga and Cutler, 1978; Kessler, 1975) and is often characterized by extreme stress, including feelings of rejection, depression, hostility, bitterness, loneliness, ambivalence, guilt, failure, confusion, disorganization, and sometimes relief (Salts, 1979). In addition, this is the time when the individual begins to focus more on oneself and starts the process of becoming an autonomous social individual (Bohannan, 1970; Kessler, 1975).

The stress experienced during separation may be the result of several factors, including the numerous and dramatic changes in one's life. These include legal procedures; concern about jobs, children, family, and friends; loss of family activities and habit systems; the need to learn new roles and behaviors; and loss of a love object (Kessler, 1975; Krantzler, 1973; Salts, 1979; Weiss, 1975). These problems are often intensified by severe economic hardships (Pearlin and Johnson, 1977).

The ambiguity of this stage can also contribute to the degree of stress; one is not really married and not really single.

> In divorce, the relationships between the ex-spouses are at least spelled out in part by the decree itself. The parties are free to find substitutes for each other.... The situation has become officially defined.... The legal rights and obligations are definite.... In separation this is usually not so. [Goode, 1956: 173]

The exception to this ambiguity may be spouses who sue for legal separation. It is more often the wife who take this action so that financial support for herself and her children can be established. In addition, as previously mentioned, legal separation is sometimes a substitute for divorce.

Instead of extreme stress, some individuals report that their emotional state improves after separation (Albrecht, 1980; Spanier and Lachman, 1979), and they view this period as having a potential for growth (Chiriboga, 1979). However, the euphoria often alternates with separation distress and is likely to disappear suddenly if the individual suffers rejection or a serious failure in a subsequent relationship.

FACTORS AFFECTING SEPARATION DISTRESS

Several factors influence the effects of separation on individuals and are closely related to those that also effect adjustment (see Chapter 4). Others, however, appear to be unique to the period of separation.

Who Initiated the Separation

The person who initiated the separation and divorce has been viewed as having a distinct advantage, as he or she have been able to work through the pain of the detachment process prior to being separated (Kessler, 1975). The person who did not seek the separation and divorce often feels angry and experiences feelings of abandonment, helplessness, bewilderment, and inadequacy. However, the person who initiated the separation may also experience intense guilt about hurting the spouse (Kessler, 1975; Weiss, 1975).

Expected vs. Unexpected Separation

Separation distress appears to be greater when it is unexpected and the individual is opposed to the separation (Spanier and Casto, 1979). These situations may also result in intense anger focused on the spouse who initiated the separation (Weiss, 1975).

The Length of Separation

The clinical research of Krantzler (1973), Wallerstein and Kelly (1980), and Weiss (1975) suggests the length of time in the separation process is related to the amount of distress experienced. For example, Melichar and Chiriboga (1985) found that women who took their time in moving from the decision to separate to separation, but who then quickly filed for divorce, experienced less separation distress. In addition, women who took their time between both sets of milestones were found to be functioning more effectively. In contrast, women who moved quickly from the decision to separate to separation experienced a greater degree of separation distress.

Length of Time Married

Separations taking place before a couple has been married two years appear to produce less separation distress. It takes about two years for people to become emotionally and socially integrated into their marriage and marital roles (Weiss, 1975). After that point, additional years of marriage seem to make little difference; a person married for 2 years will experience the same amount of separation distress over the loss of marital roles as someone married 10 years. This relationship between time married and separation distress suggests that distress is part of a fundamental process involving the disruption of emotional bonds of adult individuals (Brown et al., 1980).

Reasons for Separation

The reasons for the separation are also related to the amount of separation distress experienced. For example, those reasons that reflect upon the respondent's self-esteem and feelings about ending the marriage (extramarital sex, sexual problems due to health, sexual problems due to anger, and physical and psychological abuse) are related to greater stress. In contrast, reasons for the separation that reflect irritation with the spouse or the relationship are associated with a sense of relief (Kitson, 1985).

Sex Differences in the Separation Experience

Men and women appear to react to marital separation in different ways. In general, men are more vulnerable to separation than women (Chiriboga and Cutler, 1978). This vulnerability may stem from the tendency for men in American society to deny or suppress their emotional problems. Men often use buffers such as work or excessive social activity as a means of avoiding the emotional problems engendered by separation (Krantzler, 1973; Wallerstein and Kelly, 1977; Weiss, 1975).

Men experience a lower overall sense of well-being and are less happy and more restless than women, especially during the pre-decision period (Chiriboga and Cutler, 1978; Goode, 1956). Men's greater discomfort may indicate that they are less prepared to cope with object loss and experience greater difficulty in getting over a previous attachment (Krantzler, 1973). In contrast, after separation, women tend to be angrier, prouder, more uneasy about things, and experience greater emotional turmoil (Chiriboga and Cutler, 1978). Women are also viewed as being more tough-minded in their emotional lives and as not having or not being willing to use avenues of escape from their emotions. Rather, they meet their emotional needs head-on, and while they may reach an emotional low immediately after separation, they recover more quickly than men (Krantzler, 1973).

Sex-Role Orientation

The responses to separation distress are also affected by the sex-role orientations of men and women; greater interdependence during marriage may be associated with greater stress after separation (Hunt, 1966; Hunt and Hunt, 1977). In addition, Goode (1956) and Weiss (1975) also suggested that more traditional sex roles within marriage may be related to subsequent adjustment. Although our society has attributed instrumental or task-oriented activities to men and the expressive or socioemotional behaviors to women, androgynous behavior patterns are more adaptive than either traditional male or female behaviors—especially during times of major stress (Bem, 1977). Chiriboga and Thurnher (1980) concluded that a history of androgynous marital roles and separate interests and hobbies by spouses were associated with the well-being of separated persons (except men over age 40). In addition, Bloom and Clement (1984) found women with more traditional sex-role attitudes (more family-oriented) experienced poorer adjustment whereas women with higher self-orientation experienced better postseparation adjustment.

CONTINUED ATTACHMENT AFTER SEPARATION

In addition to the stress related to adjustments in a person's social, economic, and parental roles, separated persons also experience stress because of ambivalent feelings toward their spouse (Bloom and Hodges, 1981; Goode, 1956; Spanier and Casto, 1979; Weiss, 1975). It appears that in unhappy marriages, most of the components of love fade—sometimes to be replaced by their opposites. In this way, trust may change to mistrust, idealization to disrespect, liking to disdain. Attachment, however, seems to persist (Weiss, 1975).

This emotional ambivalence is a function of the erosion of love and the persistence of attachment. Weiss (1975) compared the attachment between spouses to the parent-child attachment described by Bowlby (1969). This attachment has an "imprinted quality"; once established, it is extraordinarily resistant to dissipation. Furthermore, the persistence of attachment feelings can result in the psychological and physical symptoms that have been termed *separation distress*.

Evidence of the persistence of attachment was described by Krantzler (1973) in his discussion of the difficulty in letting go of his marital relationship. During the early months, he saw his wife for many reasons—legal questions, support for the children, visitation arrangements, division of household property, and so forth. However, he realized he manufactured reasons to see her; he did not want to bring the curtain down on his marriage.

During separation, people may feel compelled to reestablish contact with their spouse; they telephone or drive by where the spouse lives or create reasons for interaction. They feel drawn to the spouse, even when a new relationship is established, because the new individual does not substitute for the original partner. This bond appears to be unrelated to liking, admiration, or respect.

TELLING FAMILY AND FRIENDS

Separated people are forced to inform the significant people in their lives that they are separated and are no longer functioning as a couple. This is part of the process of establishing a new lifestyle, and friends and family play an important role. While one might assume that these people may be consistently supportive, this is not always the case.

Telling Family

Contact with relatives may increase during the first few months after divorce (Ahrons and Bowman, 1981), and these kin play a vital role in the process of adjusting to separation (Spanier and Hanson, 1981). In spite of this important role, people are usually very reluctant to tell their relatives they are separated. In fact, some persons are so uncomfortable with this task that, instead of telling their relatives, they remain in an unsatisfactory marriage long after they would otherwise have divorced (Weiss, 1975).

Newly separated individuals assume the news will shock and sadden their parents. Because relatives are usually not told about a couple's private life, this is often true. Because individuals anticipate questions, perhaps blame, or even pleas to reconcile, they may postpone the news until they can personally see their relatives. Separated individuals usually try to tell all members of their family at the same time; however, they may find it easier to first tell a sibling—who then will tell their parents (Weiss, 1975).

In many marriages, the wife has been responsible for maintaining contact with the husband's family as well as her own. As a result, there is a closer attachment between the husband's parents and the wife than between the wife's parents and the husband (Ahrons and Bowman, 1981; Anspach, 1976; Spicer and Hampe, 1975). In these cases, it sometimes becomes the wife's responsibility to inform both families. No matter how objective she may attempt to be regarding the reasons for the separation, she tends to describe the reasons for the break from her perspective (Weiss, 1975). Therefore, the husband's parents may not be informed of their son's viewpoint as to why he and his wife separated.

Family Responses

How the separating person behaves during this time may set the tone for how other family members deal with the situation (Kaslow and Hyatt, 1981). Reactions of family members vary widely and may include being solicitous and anxious to help, gently or harshly condemning, angry, or choosing not to get involved (Bohannan, 1970). However, for parents of the divorcing couple, it often results in emotional trauma (Johnson and Vinick, 1981). The response to the separation depends largely on the family's definition of divorce as a tragedy, failure, irresponsibility, correction of a mistake, or a chance for self-growth (Weiss, 1975).

Many family members will expect an explanation, and possibly a report of the sequence of events that led to the separation. In this case, it is up to the separated person to decide how much to tell; some couples may even plan in advance what they will say. Parents often look for tangible reasons for the divorce, such as adultery and cruelty. However, due to societal changes, the primary reasons for divorce have changed from clearly identifiable reasons to those that deal with personal fulfillment or incompatibility (Levinger, 1979a). Therefore, parents may have a much harder time understanding why the marriage is ending (Weiss, 1975).

Relatives often feel they have a right to evaluate one another's behavior. Parents may assume the right to comment on the divorce, to criticize it, to disapprove or approve it—intensifying divorce distress for their children (Goode, 1956). Parents may also feel the divorce is a disgrace to family pride, and sibling rivalries may be reawakened by the separation (Weiss, 1975).

Some parents blame themselves for the separation and experience feelings of disappointment, failure, and helplessness (Brown, 1976). They may worry about having failed to prepare their child for marriage or having permitted or encouraged their child to make an unwise marriage. Parents may also fear and/or regret the lost contact with their son- or daughter-in-law and grandchildren (Johnson and Vinick, 1981). In addition, siblings may fear this separation suggests a familial tendency toward marital separation (Weiss, 1975).

A minority of parents and siblings completely condemn the separated individual (Bohannan, 1970; Levinger, 1965). These families offer little or no support to the separated person (Spanier and Lachman, 1979). In contrast, the reaction of most families (84% in Spanier and Casto's [1979] study) is generally supportive during this period, and there is a high incidence of interaction with, and support from, kin. With regard to financial aid, separated individuals rely primarily on parents and rarely on other kin. They do, however, rely on both parents and siblings for moral support (Spanier and Hanson, 1981).

The relation of this support to individual adjustment during separation is unclear. Individuals who do not receive support have been reported to experience increased difficulties, especially in emotional adjustment (Goode, 1956; Spanier et al., 1979). Raschke (1979) found that the more involved separated people were with their families, the less stress they experienced. In contrast, Spanier and Hanson (1981) found that adjustment to marital separation was either not contingent on or was negatively related to kin interaction and support. They attributed this finding to the possibility that adjustment to separation may actually occur before the separation occurs, making it unlikely that relatives are able to give support at the most critical time. In addition, the interaction and support that kin offer may be tempered by evaluation, disapproval, criticism, or intrusions.

Returning to Live at Home

Kin may provide help by offering services such as child care, providing companionship, or lending money (Furstenberg, 1976; Ross and Sawhill, 1975; Weiss, 1975). Kin support may be welcome because it often does not involve some of the burdensome obligations of support from other sources (i.e., interest on borrowed money). Such help may be superior to support from friends or coworkers because of the absence of an obligation to return aid after receiving it (Spanier and Hanson, 1981).

Sometimes parents offer a separated child the refuge of their home. Although both sexes are invited—the offer is made more often, and with greater insistence, to daughters. Parental motivations for this invitation may be more complex than a simple desire to help. Parents may feel the separation is the result of their inadequate parenting and that by having their child at home they will have another chance. Parents may also hope to provide their grandchildren with a more stable home environment (Weiss, 1975).

Regardless of the parents' motivation, there are disadvantages and advantages for the separated child. The disadvantages of returning home, especially for a daughter, include (a) the parents' viewing her attempt at adulthood as a failure or (b) parents' wanting to nurture and protect her, thereby directing her life. Therefore, if a woman returns home, it threatens her autonomy, and this may result in conflict between her and her parents (Weiss, 1975).

The advantages of a separated woman returning home could include the temporary relief from responsibility, reduced financial strains, and decreased guilt about neglecting her children. Grandparents can provide help with children, allowing the separated woman to continue or to pursue other adult roles, such as employment or education. Returning home may also help fill the separated person's need for social interaction (Goode, 1956; Raschke, 1979; Weiss, 1975).

Men more often view a move back home as practical, convenient, and temporary. They become less absorbed into their parents' household, and they subsequently seem to encounter fewer conflicts. However, returning home still symbolizes a return to an earlier stage of life, and "there is a loss of status in moving from head of a household to occupant of a room in the parents' household" (Weiss, 1975: 142).

Telling Friends

The reaction of friends to the news of marital separation is as varied as the reaction of family members. Krantzler (1973) found his personal experience to be gratifying, as many were delighted to hear from him and were truly concerned. Others, however, were uninterested in maintaining contact because he was only one-half a social unit. He finally realized he had to supplement old friends with new friends.

Telling friends is difficult because it is a public declaration about one's private life (Weiss, 1975). In addition, because each spouse is inclined to develop his or her account of the reasons for the separation, friends are likely to hear very different and conflicting stories from each spouse.

It is unclear how coworkers should be informed about the separation. People often feel they must report this major life event in order to maintain comfortable relationships with coworkers. In general, these relationships—as well as others that are based on an individual's interests or qualities (skill at bridge, fishing friends)—continue relatively unchanged by the separation (Weiss, 1975).

In contrast, those friendships that depended on one's marital status can be devastated as a result of separation. Separated persons may no longer be similar enough to married friends to fit into couple-oriented social events; they may change their circumstances (become employed or move) so that getting together with friends is difficult; they may have new concerns (financial or loneliness); or both parties may desire something different in friendship.

Some of the married couples who had been friends of the separated couple will ally themselves with one or the other of the spouses after the separation. However, in more amicable separations, husbands and wives may desire that both spouses retain their former friends.

Weiss (1975) reported three phases likely to occur in a separated person's relationships with friends. These include *rallying round, idiosyncratic reactions,* and *mutual withdrawal:*

(1) First phase: rallying round. The immediate response of friends is likely to be a desire to help. They will invite the separated person to visit or respect his or her privacy, and not inquire as to what went wrong. If the separated person wants to talk, these friends will listen and may offer advice. When friends want to help, they should be advised as to what they can do. For example, they may help in those areas in which the separated spouse is not proficient (Johnson, 1976).

(2) Second phase: idiosyncratic reactions. During this phase, friends recognize the individual is separated, and therefore different. This suggests the separated person is moving to a new lifestyle in which he or she will be confronted with the freedom and anxieties of being alone. Consequently, while some friends continue to be welcoming, others feel burdened by the emotions of the separated person, or frightened, as if separation were a communicable disease. Still others react with envy, admiration, or curiosity about the separated person.

(3) Third phase: mutual withdrawal. The third phase involves the mutual withdrawal between separated persons and couples who had been their friends when they were married. There is no explicit ending to these relationships—rather, they are allowed to fade. Separated persons may imagine themselves to be rejected by these couples, but continued interaction may also be painful, as it forces the separated to recognize how much has changed.

Eventually, the separated person is likely to establish a new network of friends (Krantzler, 1973). This network may include one or two married couples, same-sex members of married couples, an intimate friend, and/or less close unmarried friends. The separated person increasingly spends time with others who are divorced or separated, often including a person of the opposite sex who is "just a friend" (Weiss, 1975).

RECONCILIATION

It is often assumed that the process of separation leads to divorce. However, this is not always true; Weiss (1975) has proposed that less than one-half of all separations end in divorce.

The exact number or proportion of couples who experience separation and reconciliation in their married life is not known. Several researchers, however, have investigated this process. Kitson et al., (1983) found 23% of the divorces filed in the Cleveland, Ohio, suburbs in 1974-1975 were withdrawn or dismissed, and Levinger (1966) reported that 20% to 30% of suits for divorce in his study were withdrawn, with couples apparently returning to their marriages.

Reconciliation does not appear to be distributed equally among all segments of the separated population. Couples most likely to reconcile include those with higher levels of education and income; those who have been separated for a shorter period of time, those in which the wives have lower incomes, couples with few or no children, younger couples, couples in which the wife is employed, couples with fewer grounds for divorce, and couples in which the wife is older than her husband (Bloom et al., 1977; Kitson et al., 1983; Kitson and Langlie, 1984; Levinger, 1979b).

Levinger (1979a, 1979b) applied his theory of attractions and barriers to 300 couples who dismissed their divorce suits and 300 couples who finalized their divorces. Because wives were the plaintiffs in 80% of these cases, Levinger concluded that they made an economic comparison between their marriages' internal attractions (husband's income and security) and external attractions (wife's earnings and employment opportunities). Based on this comparison, they determined whether or not to reconcile with their spouses.

In order to test Levinger's theory, Kitson et al. (1983) compared 568 couples who had reconciled or completed their divorces. They hypothesized that couples withdraw their petitions for divorce when they recognize the rewards in their marriage are greater than the costs they encounter outside of it; therefore, the alternatives are unattractive. They were able to accurately predict reconciliation using only structural and demographic variables, but concluded their study supported an exchange model of divorce.

Having dependent children has been viewed as increasing the cost of divorce, especially for women (Brandwein et al., 1974). Kitson et al. (1983), however, found having children made couples less likely to reconcile. They concluded that having children may make staying in an unsatisfactory marriage too costly because parents may not want to rear their children in this atmosphere.

It is assumed the period of separation affords spouses an opportunity to evaluate the costs and rewards of divorce or continuation of their marriage. During this time, anticipated lowered costs and increased rewards may not materialize, and, in fact, costs may increase and rewards may decrease. If outcomes during the separation fall below the known alternatives offered by the marriage, a person will be less attracted to separation and drawn back into the marital relationship (Wright, 1985).

Resources may also change during the period of separation. For example, Levinger (1979a, 1979b) found couples with greater income disparity were more likely to reconcile. This has been attributed to the partner with fewer resources (more often women) not being able to find employment, and/or the partner with more resources (more often men) finding the costs of maintaining two households or the redistribution of resources as a result of the divorce settlement, reducing their resources more than they can tolerate. In either case, a spouse with fewer resources is more likely to have difficulty ending a marriage (Pearlin and Johnson, 1977) and also be more attracted to the possibility of reconciliation.

Reconciliation may result in the marriage being revitalized and attachments reactivated. In fact, the separation period may serve as a "cooling off" and reassessment period, confirming for the couple that they do not want to end the marriage. In contrast, it could also result in feelings of dismay at returning to an unsatisfactory relationship (Weiss, 1975).

Kitson and Langlie (1984) found that reconciled couples were not without problems. They compared reconciled couples with (a) couples who continued to finalize their divorce and (b) married couples. They found that the reconciled couples mentioned more serious marital complaints, such as alcohol or other drug use, threatened or actual physical abuse, desertion, criminal activities, and emotional and personality problems, than the divorced group. These reconciled couples also had higher scores on subjective distress indicators and more psychophysiological complaints than did the divorced or married comparison groups.

It would appear that if a couple decides to reconcile, they should realize their problems won't disappear. Rather, they have to be ready to take the necessary steps, possibly including seeking professional help, in order to rebuild their relationship.

SUMMARY

Separation is more prevalent than divorce and may reflect a normal event in a generally satisfying marriage. For other couples, however, it is a very stressful time in the divorce process. This process starts with one or both spouses experiencing disillusionment with their marriage and culminates in actual separation of the spouses.

One of the most difficult tasks separated spouses must do is inform friends and relatives. Although one might assume these people would be supportive, this is not always the case. Rather, it depends largely on their definition of divorce as a tragedy, failure, irresponsibility, correction of a mistake, or a chance for self-growth.

Less than one-half of all separations end in divorce. Many couples, after separating, recognize that the rewards in their marriage are greater than the costs they would encounter outside it. Consequently, they decide to reconcile. While reconciliation may result in the marriage being revitalized and attachments reactivated, it may also result in feelings of dismay at returning to an unsatisfactory relationship.

REVIEW QUESTIONS

1. What are the characteristics of each stage of the separation process?
2. Describe the reaction of friends and relatives to the news that a couple is separated. How would these reactions help or hinder a person during the period of separation?
3. What factors appear to be most highly related to separation distress?
4. Apply social exchange theory to account for the decision of a couple to reconcile. What are the advantages and disadvantages of reconciliation?

SUGGESTED PROJECTS

1. Find out your state's separation requirement for married persons who have filed for divorce.
2. Interview mental health practitioners regarding the stress they have seen their clients experience as the result of marital separation.
3. Collect five articles from popular magazines related to separation distress. Identify common themes that run through these articles.
4. Interview local attorneys or legal aid offices for patterns of reconciliation they see in their clients. Are there any types of relationships that they see as more likely to reconcile?

CHAPTER

4

Adjusting to Divorce

There is nothing funny or easy about divorce. No short cuts, no magic formulas, no quick and easy solutions to the emotional turmoil that inevitably follows the dissolution of a marriage. It is a savage emotional journey, and where it will end nobody knows, at least for a while. [Trafford, 1982: xi]

DIVORCE IS ORDINARILY VIEWED as a painful, stressful, and crisis-producing event in one's life (Bloom, Asher, and White, 1978; Hetherington, Cox, and Cox, 1978; Holmes and Rahe, 1976; Hunt and Hunt, 1977; Weiss, 1975). The consequences of divorce typically begin long before the separation, and create the need for the numerous adjustments divorced people must make. In particular, negative consequences (e.g., lowered economic status, changes in social life, role redefinitions, changes in kinship interaction) make adjustment difficult (Raschke, 1987).

It has historically been assumed that a person was adjusted to divorce if she or he remarried or ceased all contact with the former spouse. A better definition is:

an ability to develop an identity for oneself that is not tied to the status of being married or to the ex-spouse and an ability to function adequately in the role responsibilities of daily life—home, family, work, and leisure time. [Kitson and Raschke, 1981: 16]

ADJUSTMENT AS A PROCESS

Adjustment is a developmental process usually taking from two to five years (Weiss, 1975), and it involves many areas of life, including one's daily habits, personal identity, economic status, sexual and social relationships, relationships with children and extended kin, residence, and role redefinition (Raschke and Barringer, 1977; Smart, 1979).

Adjustment to divorce has been measured using several methodologies. Several researchers (Spanier and Hanson, 1981) have used measures of variables descriptive of adjustment, that is, self-esteem, satisfaction with life, locus-of-control, as well as those that measure health and psychological functioning. Divorce adjustment has also been measured directly by scales designed to tap various dimensions of the divorce adjustment process, for example, how one is functioning in various life roles. However, these measures often assess more negative than positive aspects of divorce adjustment, and thus emphasize characteristics of being "unadjusted" (Granvold et al., 1979; Raschke, 1987). In addition, several "loss" models have been introduced to describe an individual's acceptance of the reality of divorce and development of a new lifestyle. For example, Kessler (1975) described the stages involved in adjusting to divorce after separation as mourning and recovering.

Mourning

The mourning process, which aids in helping a person rid her-or himself of the ghost of the former spouse, usually follows separation. If mourning does not happen at this time, it is inevitable that it will occur at a later point in time. It may involve anger, hurt, loneliness, and feelings of helplessness.

Anger. Anger may focus on anything, but is generally directed toward the former spouse and often takes the form of irritability, loss of patience, increased rigidity, and increased demands. While some anger is a healthy emotional behavior, some people also experience dysfunctional anger. Dysfunctional anger is destructive and results in power struggles over children, property, visitation rights, child support, and possibly vengeance, which is indicative of unresolved conflicts. In contrast, anger that is an outgrowth of frustration and hurt is normal and fills a vacuum created by emotional detachment. This latter type of anger is a common way of protecting oneself from the devastating feeling of separation.

Depression. While anger involves outward blame, depression involves blaming oneself. The sadness in depression not only allows one to deal with present losses but also prepares one for future losses.

> I have lost a loved one, a set of friends, the esteem of my family, social approval and something I once enjoyed. I will probably lose some

financial security, more comfortable habits, and some self-esteem from being respected. [Kessler, 1975: 39]

Recovery

Restoration and relief. This period occurs when a person realizes the marriage is over and a degree of objectivity about the former spouse returns. In contrast to looking back, the divorced person now concentrates on personal growth. Many divorced people have a difficult time admitting they are relieved. However, divorce does reduce conflict and pain between two people and sometimes frees a person from financial obligations, emotional bondage, and lengthy legal commitments.

The awareness of this relief may create an almost adolescent state of new beginning with the same anxieties. The divorced individual may overreact by vengefully pursuing previous areas of deprivation, for example, sex, travel, fun, or clothes. This period of overreaction may also include "the clutch." The divorced person finds a warm, under-standing, compassionate person—and wants to stay with that person. Because the other person feels overwhelmed by the divorced person's extreme dependency, she or he usually terminates the relationship, leaving the divorced person feeling demolished. However, these reactions will generally be replaced—often because of finances or limits of energy—by a more comfortable and integrated balance.

Exploration and hard work. This stage is characterized by a disappearance of the anxious floundering and the presence of a recommitment to one's life and goals. The divorced person sets realistic goals and implements a plan to reach these goals. In addition, the person is ready for a new relationship based on personal strength, rather than weakness. At this stage, the divorced person is more approachable and better able to receive and give kindness and compliments. "Now at the end of the divorce process, you have changed from being stymied to being strengthened by it" (Kessler, 1975: 44).

COPING WITH DIVORCE

For some people, divorce is a very positive life event. There have been reports of improved health status after divorce (Spanier and Lachman, 1979), and a sizable proportion (17-33%) of divorced persons have described their divorce as relatively painless or resulting in only slight emotional disturbance (Albrecht, 1980; Goode, 1956). For these persons, divorce resolves a stressful situation (e.g., a marriage character-ized by abuse) and leads to a new sense of competence and control, development of better relationships, and freedom to develop one's own interests (Brown et al., 1976). Ultimately, divorce can promote positive change by confronting a person with opportunities to develop new and adaptive ways of dealing with life (Weingarten, 1985). For these individuals, divorce may be viewed as

> a normal process with specific tasks to be mastered, recognizable stresses to be dealt with, and satisfaction and goals to be sought for. Like any other life crisis, it is to be avoided when possible; when it occurs, it can be dealt with as a means of achieving growth toward a more satisfying way of life. [Brown et al., 1976: 212]

DIVORCE AND STRESS

For most people, however, the dissolution of a marriage results in at least some pain and stress. Divorce has, in fact, been described as one of the most stressful life changes a person can experience (Holmes and Rahe, 1976). Several studies have substantiated this assertion. For example, Weiss (1975) reported that divorce created extreme stress; Hetherington, Cox, and Cox (1978) reported a state of near chaos in divorced homes one year after divorce; and Goode (1956) reported almost two-thirds of his sample experienced moderate to high levels of emotional distress sometime during the divorce process.

Divorce stressors can be divided into the following categories: (a) social, (b) psychological, and (c) behavioral (Pearlin and Schooler, 1978).

(1) Social stressors include disruptions in relationships with family, friends, children, and the former spouse; less contact with one's children; loneliness and social isolation; lack of social norms, rites, and rituals for guidance through the divorce process; lack of role models for divorce; family redefinition difficulties; lack of recognition by social institutions of the continued interest and contact among family members; difficulty in establishing a satisfactory dating and sex life; problems with an adversary legal system (see Ahrons, 1980; Berman and Turk, 1981; Bloom et al., 1979; Goetting, 1981; Kraus, 1979; Kressel, 1980; Price-Bonham and Balswick, 1980; Rose and Price-Bonham, 1973).

(2) *Psychological stressors* include the reassessment of one's social and sex roles; feelings of anger, anxiety, ambivalence, dependence, and distress; loss of identity; feelings of unattractiveness, helplessness, and incompetence (see Berman and Turk, 1981; Bloom et al., 1979; Hetherington et al., 1976, 1978).

(3) *Behavioral stressors* include disruptions in home schedules, organization, maintenance, and finances (including lost stability of income); disruptions in time management, work efficiency, and work per-

formance; increased smoking and drinking; irregular eating and sleeping habits; failure to seek and follow through with treatment for physical problems (see Berman and Turk, 1981; Bloom et al., 1979; Buehler and Hogan, 1980; Hetherington et al., 1978; Kraus, 1979).

Physical Health

The stress resulting from the process of divorce has been linked to a variety of physical health problems (Bloom et al., 1979). The National Center for Health Statistics reported that controlling for age, premature death rates (deaths between the ages of 15 and 64) were higher for divorced men and women than for married persons, with differences being significantly greater for men than for women (Carter and Glick, 1976). Specific causes of death included cirrhosis of the liver, lung cancer, coronary heart disease, tuberculosis, diabetes, leukemia, suicide, homicide, motor accidents, and pedestrian deaths, as well as other accidental deaths. Consistent with these data, the formerly married, as compared to married individuals, are more often hospitalized, more frequently visit physicians, have more acute illnesses, including terminal cancer, have higher rates of illness and disability, and miss more days of work due to illness (Lynch, 1977; Renne, 1971; U.S. Department of Health, Education, and Welfare, 1976).

Alcoholism. Divorce has been clearly related to drinking problems. For example, among 6,000 adult admissions to the emergency service of Massachusetts General Hospital, the divorced or separated of both sexes more often had positive Breathalyzer readings (Bloom et al., 1979). In addition, disrupted marriages have been found to be related to multiple hospitalizations for acute alcohol psychoses at ages below 45 (Bloom et al., 1979).

Automobile and other accidents. The divorced are far more likely than the married or single to be involved in accidents involving fatalities. Divorced men and women, both White and non-White, average three to four times greater rates of death as a result of automobile accidents than their nondivorced counterparts (Gove, 1973). In addition, the rate of automobile-related deaths doubles during the period of time between six months before and six months after the divorce (Bloom et al., 1979). Divorced men are seven to eight times more likely to die as the result of a pedestrian accident and four to five times more likely to die from other accidents than are married men. Divorced women are three to four times as likely to die as a result of accidental deaths, and four to five times more likely to die as the result of a pedestrian accident than married women (Gove, 1973).

Suicide and homicide. The maritally disrupted are consistently found to be overrepresented among those people who die from suicide and homicide. Divorced men commit suicide almost five times more frequently than married men and divorced women three and one-half times as often as married women. In addition, divorced men commit suicide approximately one and one-half times more frequently than divorced women. These suicidal behaviors are generally attributed to the losses and disturbances in severing the marital relationship (Stack, 1980).

The risk of death by homicide is higher for the divorced than other marital status groups. For example, among the divorced, White men are murdered seven to eight times more frequently and White women between four and five times more frequently than their married counterparts. In addition, among divorced non-Whites the risk of being murdered is twice as high among women and three times as high among men than non-White men and women who are not divorced (Gove, 1973).

Mental Health

Divorced and separated persons are consistently overrepresented among those evidencing psychological disturbances (Bloom et al., 1979; Ladbrook, 1976). More specifically, both local and national figures reveal that regardless of the type of facility considered, admission rates for psychological disturbances were lowest among the married, intermediate among the widowed, and highest among the divorced and separated. The ratio of admission into outpatient facilities for divorced and separated persons compared to those of married persons varies from 7-to-1 to 22-to-1 for males, and from 3-to-1 to 8-to-1 for females. Furthermore, this relationship holds across both sexes and for Blacks and Whites. In addition, for those persons seeking help at various facilities, other divorcing or divorced persons have reported feelings of intense depression (Goode, 1956; Weiss, 1975), as well as feelings of guilt, shame, or fears of the future to a degree that is viewed as almost pathological (Gray, 1978).

Explanations for Divorce and Health Problems

It is difficult to establish a clear cause-effect relationship between mental and physical health problems and divorce. The lack of longitudinal research in this area results in a vacuum of information regarding whether or not these symptoms existed prior to the divorce (Menaghan, 1985). Further, it is possible other factors, for example, lack of health care, lower social class, and lack of proper nutrition, predispose persons to both divorce and ill health (Goetting, 1981). In addition, divorced persons historically have been viewed as deviant. If society assumes the only way to live is married and in a nuclear family, it stands to reason that those persons who deviate from this norm will be viewed as "abnormal." This stigma alone may result in stress-related health problems.

Four theories have been postulated to explain the differences in health status between married and divorced persons (Bloom et al., 1979; Kraus, 1979; Pearlin and Johnson, 1977):

(1) *Selectivity:* Health problems reduce the likelihood of physically and emotionally handicapped persons' marrying as well as the likelihood they will remain married.

(2) *Postmarital disability:* Emotional or physical problems arising subsequent to marriage increase the likelihood that a marriage will be terminated by divorce; that is, marriage can be sustained only by persons who remain "fit."

(3) *Role theory:* The security of being married and living with one's spouse reduces vulnerability to a variety of diseases and emotional disorders.

(4) *Stress theory:* Divorce is a life stressor that can precipitate physical and/or emotional disorders in people.

While both selectivity theory and role theory have been criticized in explaining the relationship between ill-health and divorce (Gove, 1973), stress theory has been adopted by many researchers to conceptualize this relationship (Brown and Fox, 1978; Kraus, 1979). Therefore, divorce is increasingly viewed as a life crisis involving a series of social and psychological stresses. It is a crisis that upsets an "individual's steady state, his or her everyday equilibrium, which cannot be dealt with by his or her usual coping mechanisms" (Kraus, 1979: 111). The reaction to divorce may include both short-term and long-term reactions. The short-term reaction may be a temporary state of personality disorganization that is often mistaken for psychopathology, in contrast to the long-term reaction that culminates in a wide range of outcomes—from psychopathology to strengthened functioning (Kraus, 1979).

MEN, WOMEN, AND ADJUSTING TO DIVORCE

There appears to be an ongoing debate over which sex "has it worse" in divorce. Findings relative to this question are contradictory. In one study comparing an urban population with small town and small city participants in Parents Without Partners, females reported greater stress in the urban sample whereas males reported greater stress in the small town and small city group (Raschke and Barringer, 1977). In other studies (for example, DeFrain and Eirick, 1981; Spanier and Casto, 1979; Weiss, 1975), few or no differences were found between men and women in their responses to divorce. This similarity is attributed to the fact that both men and women must deal with pragmatic concerns, interpersonal and social problems, and family-related stresses (Berman and Turk, 1981). The latter may originate from several areas, including the negative interaction that took place between the spouses preceding, during, and following the divorce (Berman and Turk, 1981); the continued attachment and resulting feelings of ambivalence toward the former spouse; and the disruption of regular child-rearing practices and communication (Hetherington et al., 1976; Weiss, 1975). In addition, both sexes have reported difficulty in areas such as home repair and maintenance, work, household organization, and finances, as well as feelings of being overwhelmed and not having enough time to do everything (Berman and Turk, 1981; Brandwein et al., 1974; Goode, 1956; Hetherington et al., 1976, 1978; Mendes, 1976).

While the emotional and personal problems facing men and women who have experienced divorce are similar, their patterns of reaction may be different. Several studies have provided evidence that men are more debilitated than women as a result of divorce (Gove, 1973), and experience lower levels of adjustment (Price-Bonham et al., 1982; Wallerstein, 1986; Zeiss et al., 1980). However, while emotional problems are initially more severe for men, women may experience more long-term divorce distress (Hetherington et al., 1978). These differences appear to be the consequence of socialization for gender-related social roles and coping styles and are exacerbated by economic problems and responsibility for children. It is expected that as sex-role socialization becomes less rigid, the differences experienced by divorced men and women will be outweighed by the similarities (Brown and Fox, 1978).

Impact of Divorce on Women

Because of differential sex role socialization, it can be assumed that men and women may experience a "his" and "her" divorce. Historically, when women married they withdrew from the labor force and focused their lives on their husbands and children—gaining a primary identity from these roles. These women can be expected to have especially difficult problems as the result of divorce because they have been socialized into dependency roles and may still depend on others for answers in social, economic, and emotional areas of life. In addition, these women may view divorce as failure, that is, failure in the area that has been their most important source of identity and self-esteem (Bardwick, 1971). Therefore, if a woman is too heavily invested in her role as wife, her transformation into an independent and self-sufficient person will require denying the value of sacrificing personal independence and expressions of selfhood that she made in order to live according to the rules of married life (Krantzler, 1973).

Women with more egalitarian sex-role attitudes and expectations will have a less difficult time if divorced (Brown and Manela, 1977a; Granvold et al., 1979). If a woman has maintained a strong sense of identity and is involved in roles apart from her family, her losses, as a result of divorce, will not be as devastating:

> A woman, I would venture, with self-identity based on her own unique accomplishments, personality, creativity, and leadership outside of marriage would not be traumatized as severely as a woman with just a marital self-identity when divorce hits. Men are no different on that dimension. They have just had more time to practice, more reinforcement for practicing, and more opportunities to achieve self- and career-identities. [Kessler, 1975: 170]

Almost completely absent in the literature on divorce is recognition of the opportunities for divorced women (Mitchell, 1983). Women may mourn the loss of the wife role and, especially in the case of the single parent, may be burdened with practical and economic demands that may lead to lowered self-esteem, feelings of helplessness, and psychological distress. At the same time, divorce can also provide women with opportunities to realize their potential for growth and to exercise new levels of autonomy and feelings of personal competence and esteem. In fact, some divorced women report increased competence and higher self-esteem as a result of learning to manage alone (Wallerstein and Kelly, 1980), and an improved quality of life—even a decade after divorcing (Wallerstein, 1986).

Several authors have reported racial differences in women's adjusting to divorce. Black women who are heads of households appear to cope better than their White counterparts (Geerkin and Gove, 1974). In a study of low-income mothers in a southeastern metropolitan area, both Black and White mothers reported large decreases in income. Black mothers, however, perceived themselves as experiencing significantly less distress than White mothers. Furthermore, White mothers reported greater feelings of loneliness, being hassled, and having inadequate time, whereas Black mothers reported greater social supports (Raschke, 1979).

Older women. Older women have a more difficult time with divorce adjustment than do younger women (Chiriboga et al., 1978; Wallerstein, 1986). These women are less likely to remarry, have fewer financial resources, are more anxious about living alone, suffer more acute loneliness, and exhibit more psychosomatic illnesses than do younger women (Langelier and Deckert, 1980; Wallerstein, 1986; Woodard et al., 1980).

This greater difficulty in adjustment is at least partially attributed to women losing the social support system that they had in marriage. This loss is particularly evident in social situations, decision making, and dealing with finances (Woodard et al., 1980). Older women are particularly vulnerable to problems in their social lives because of the societal message that physical aging in women is not sexually attractive (Cleveland, 1979). They are also confronted with a new social life and lifestyle that is characterized by changing and conflicting values (Langelier and Deckert, 1980), and may be viewed by men in their age cohort as a threat because of the similarity to their former wives. For this reason, interest of younger men may precipitate a revitalization of their youthful feelings of desirability and excitement (Cleveland, 1979).

Older women may also experience more adjustment problems following divorce because they may have experienced a longer period of marital conflict than younger women. They also have more established marriage-based lifestyles, and subsequently find it more difficult to develop a new personal identity and new social relationships (Nelson, 1981). In addition, older women are more likely to have been socialized into rigid stereotyped gender roles and hence have a harder time breaking out of this mold.

Impact of Divorce on Men

There have been few studies that have focused on the impact of divorce on men. However, there is some evidence that indicates divorce constitutes a severe emotional impact for them (Albrecht et al., 1983; Weiss, 1975). In fact, divorced men may exhibit more symptoms of emotional and physical disturbances than divorced women (Bloom and Caldwell, 1981; Gove, 1973; White and Bloom, 1981). This gender difference has been attributed to men's tendency to deny their dependency needs and their feelings about the possible loss of their children, friends, home, possessions, and sometimes status (Dreyfus, 1979). In addition, men are viewed as having a greater need for marriage than women, and therefore suffer more from its absence (Bernard, 1972).

FACTORS RELATED TO ADJUSTMENT

In addition to gender, there are other factors that are related to how men and women adjust to divorce. Some of these variables, such as age, length of marriage, presence of children, the divorce decision, the legal system, and length of separation, cannot be modified and are outside a person's control. Other variables that can be modified include socioeconomic status, support systems, and psychological resources (Raschke, 1987). The following is a discussion of major factors that researchers have found to be related to postdivorce adjustment.

Children

Findings are inconsistent regarding how children affect adjustment following divorce, since they can function as both assets and liabilities. The presence of children, however, generally necessitates major adjustments for both custodial and noncustodial parents (Bloom and Hodges, 1981), and research does indicate that more children and younger children result in more trauma for women (Goode, 1956; Pais and White, 1979; Pearlin and Johnson, 1977). Even two years after divorce, male children (especially teenagers) appear to create more difficulties and increase postdivorce stress for mothers (Berman and Turk, 1981; Hetherington et al., 1976, 1978).

In contrast, children may function as a resource following divorce; it may be children who keep parents going (Weiss, 1975) and subsequently reduce stress (Raschke and Barringer, 1977; Raschke and Marroni, 1977). Absence of children, however, is related to more positive postdivorce adjustment (Myers, 1976).

Age and Length of Marriage

Age and length of marriage are closely related. In general, the longer a person has been married, the more difficult it is to adjust to divorce (Chiriboga, 1982; Hetherington et al., 1978; Wallerstein, 1986). The impact of a divorce at midlife and later is more devastating than in youth. The recovery period takes longer, and finding a new partner is more difficult (Berardo, 1982). Persons who divorce later in life are less happy than younger persons (Bloom et al., 1979). For these individuals, long-time friends may be lost, contact with in-laws may decrease, older children taking sides may result in a loss of contact (DeShane and Brown-Wilson, 1981), avenues of sexual relationships are not as available, and finances, including pensions and retirements, may be strained or lost.

Persons who divorce after marriages of longer duration also appear to have more to relearn. Larger and more complex social networks may be threatened, and the need to revise long-term habits and lifestyles contributes to the stress (Gubrium, 1974). At the same time, there is a decreasing availability of resources with which to cope with the stressors precipitated by divorce (Lowenthal et al., 1975).

The Legal System

One of the rationales for implementation of the no-fault divorce system was to decrease the acrimony generally present in the fault system (Spanier and Anderson, 1979). This may be true, as the reduction in the number of litigious actions in California also has resulted in decreases in the hostility between spouses (Dixon and Weitzman, 1980). There are questions, however, whether no-fault divorce has actually reduced postdivorce distress, since it appears to be an economic disaster for women and children (see Chapters 5, 6, and 7). Therefore, adjustment is often more difficult because of the economic implications of no-fault divorce (Raschke, 1987).

Length of Separation

The longer the period of time since physical separation, the more positive the adjustment (Chiriboga and Cutler, 1978; Kessler, 1975; Pais and White, 1979; Raschke and Barringer, 1977). The amount of distress is highest immediately before and following separation (see Chapter 3). This may be the time when divorcing people experience the greatest emotional trauma and economic hardships (Pearlin and Johnson, 1977).

Socioeconomic Status

Economic problems are inversely related to divorce adjustment for both men and women (Spanier and Casto, 1979); the higher the income, the lower the distress (Bould, 1977). Divorce has a more detrimental economic affect on women than men (Weitzman, 1985), and for many women divorce means a drastically reduced income and/or having to enter the labor market with an absence or shortage of job skills. Being dependent on a former spouse may not alleviate this distress. Women who receive alimony are constantly reminded of their former marriage and their dependent status. In addition, sources of income make a difference in adjustment. Women on welfare have more adjustment problems (Bould, 1977; Pett, 1982); women seeking welfare following a divorce typically have less confidence in themselves and have a more negative self-concept than women who choose to seek employment in equivalent low-paying jobs (Pett, 1982). Economic independence may be one reason dual-career spouses experience less psychological trauma as a result of divorce (Rice, 1979).

Psychological Resources

Divorced persons are affected by both internal and external factors (Raschke, 1987). Higher religiosity and more frequent church attendance are related to more positive post-divorce adjustment and lower stress (Brown, 1976; Raschke and Barringer, 1977). Marked increases in programs for the divorced that churches have recently implemented may explain this relationship (Raschke, 1987). In addition, a higher tolerance for change and lower dogmatism (open minded vs. closed mindedness) are associated with lower stress (Hynes, 1979; Raschke and Marroni, 1977). Finally, preoccupation and longing for the former spouse is associated with more distress and poor adjustment (Kitson, 1982).

FORMER SPOUSE RELATIONSHIPS

Divorce does not necessarily result in the dissolution of the family system; divorce moves one from a nuclear family to a post-divorce "binuclear family" (Ahrons, 1980). This "binuclear family" involves a complex redefinition of relationships. Once family members have established ground rules for living separately, they need to clarify rules for relating within the various subsystems within the family system, that is, the coparental relationship, the parent-child relationship, and the former spouse relationship (Ahrons, 1980; Ahrons and Wallisch, 1986; Goldsmith, 1980).

The concept of family boundaries, defined by Minuchin (1974) as rules that govern the parameters of a family system, applies to both intact and divorced families. Former spouses need to establish new rules that will redefine their continuing relationship as well as their parental roles in order to ensure proper family functioning. Confusion results if these boundaries are not clear. For example, there are two separate subsystems for parents—the spousal and the parental, with considerable overlap between the two. After divorce, however, the spousal subsystem must be separated from the parental subsystem. Consequently, it is often difficult for divorced couples to define where their former-spouse relationship ends and where their parental relationship begins (Ahrons, 1980; Roberts and Price, 1985/1986).

Coparental Relationship

The coparental relationship involves two relationships: (a) the relationship a parent develops with his or her children during and after the divorce, and (b) the relationship former spouses develop with one another in regard to their children. There is little agreement regarding the ideal coparental relationship (Suarez et al., 1978). The lack of agreement is at least partially attributed to a lack of role models for couples in this situation (Ahrons, 1979). In addition, there may be conflict between former spouses because of basic differences in child rearing opinions (Goldsmith, 1980).

There is wide variation among couples in the amount of involvement relative to their children. Some couples communicate very frequently (twice or more per week) while others do not communicate at all. The amount of communication also varies by the child rearing area involved. School or medical problems result in the highest frequency of interaction, whereas everyday decisions, children's adjustment to the divorce, and child-related finances account for the lowest frequency of interaction. However, coparental interaction appears to decline significantly over time whereas noncustodial fathers' anger over child rearing issues appear to increase (Ahrons and Wallisch, 1986; Goldsmith, 1980).

Divorced parents also appear to continue the coparental relationship in activities where they spend time together with their children. These activities, which also decrease over time, generally include holidays and celebrations, eating together, and school activities; a small minority of divorced parents also visit grandparents or other relatives together (Ahrons and Wallisch, 1986; Goldsmith, 1980).

Parents sometimes express consensus about the ideal divorced parenting relationship (Schulman, 1981). Such a relationship includes open and frequent communication, cooperation, and flexibility in scheduling visits, allowing children to see parents freely, separating child rearing issues from marital issues, taking into account financial needs and limitations, and being mutually supportive and cooperative (Ahrons and Wallisch, 1986; Kressel and Deutsch, 1977). The relationship that develops between a parent and a child after divorce is crucial. Continued access to both parents has a positive influence on how children adjust to a divorce (Wallerstein and Kelly, 1980). One of the major tasks for divorced couples is to realize that divorce does not terminate parenthood and that ways must be found to ensure that children will continue to have, and be able to rely on, both parents (Schulman, 1981).

The Nonparental Relationship

Historically, much of the literature relative to former spouse relationships assumed that healthy adjustment after divorce implied termination of any relationship between the individuals (Ahrons, 1979; Rose and Price-Bonham, 1973; Spanier and Casto, 1979). However, the former spouse relationship is increasingly viewed as "in transition" rather than dissolved (Ahrons, 1979).

The former spouse relationship involves attachment, "the complex and often long-lasting affective bond between two people" (Bloom and Kindle, 1985: 375). The bonds of attachment are often exhibited through recurrent thoughts and images of the former spouse, attempts to contact or learn about him or her, feelings of missing part of oneself, and loneliness and panic (Berman, 1985; Parkes, 1973; Weiss, 1975). This continued attachment between former spouses has been repeatedly documented. Spanier and Casto (1979) found 70% of their respondents reported mild or strong attachment. Similarly, Brown et al. (1980), in their study of divorcing couples who sought court-supported counseling, found 22% of their respondents reported high, 31% reported moderate, and 47% reported low attachment. A recent longitudinal study, conducted by Kitson (1982), revealed 42% of her respondents reported low, 25% high, and 18% moderate attachment.

One reason the postdivorce relationship is difficult is the lack of defined societal roles for divorced people. This deficiency is evident in our lack of a language that describes the former spouse relationship:

> The vulgar "my ex" is all that we have to deal with the relationship that may involve twenty years and five children. We should be able to do better—and soon. [Mead, 1971: 125]

In fact, most knowledge we have regarding this relationship is based on stereotypes, that is, former spouses must be enemies, otherwise, why would they divorce (Ahrons, 1980). Therefore, couples must invent their own ways of dealing with each other.

The former spouse relationship is viewed as the "hardest to understand, and once understood, the most difficult to overcome—and consisting of four people—a man and woman suddenly strangers to each other, and the familiar husband and wife we once had been" (Krantzler, 1973: 51-52). In spite of complications, however, former spouses often remain bound to one another by children, love, hate, friendship, business matters, dependence, moral obligations, or simply habit. While children are the most common link between former spouses (Goetting, 1979), other specific reasons have been found to be property settlements, financial support, and attachment (Hetherington et al., 1978, 1979a, 1979b). In addition, former spouses may continue a relationship because of tangible connections, such as child support; this contact will remain so long as the obligations exist, thereby preserving some trace of the former familial relationship.

Divorced spouses often have difficulty breaking customary patterns of interaction. Consequently, they feel compelled to reestablish contact; these feelings may be unrelated to liking, admiration, or respect. Their interactions may occupy much time and energy and are often a continuation of previous patterns of interaction involving conflicts. While these feelings may fade over time, seeing the former spouse after the passage of years may still invoke a resurgence of fondness, anger, bitterness, and yearning—less strong, but still present (Weiss, 1975).

Ambivalence. The feelings of attachment between former spouses produce feelings of desire to reconcile and intense anger because of the spouse's role in the production of separation distress. In the short-run, former spouses may not be able to resolve these ambivalent feelings. However, in the long-run, former spouses report handling their ambivalent feelings by suppressing positive and negative feelings, alternating these feelings, or compartmentalizing the discrepant feelings (Hunt and Hunt, 1977; Spanier and Thompson, 1984; Weiss, 1975).

Sex between former spouses. An area of the former spouse relationship that has received little attention, but one that seems to remain viable for some couples after divorce, is their sexual relationship. Sexual attraction to the former mate may linger on for some people because it is safe, convenient, and habitual. Therefore, it is not uncommon for former spouses to have sexual relations (Cleveland, 1979; Hunt and Hunt, 1977). Sexual activity at this time, however, may confuse the postdivorce situation if it raises the hopes of reconciliation for one or both persons. In addition, it often results in mixed messages ("I can't stand you any longer; I find you sexually irresistible"), thereby reinforcing feelings of ambivalence.

Distrust of the former spouse relationship. Some writers are very suspicious of former spouse relationships. For example, Krantzler (1973) contended that initially "chances are slim" that former spouses can be good friends. He contended that only when a former partner feels secure as an independent person can she or he be certain expressions of friendship toward a former spouse are not unrecognized "hangovers" of emotional needs. Others have viewed continued relationships between former spouses as pathological and indicative of an inability to separate. Some psychotherapists express the sentiment that former spouses who are friends, business partners, or lovers are actually experiencing separation distress rather than realistic caring. These continuing attachments are viewed as draining energies that could be more productively spent in new relationships (Kressel and Deutsch, 1977). The best policy, according to this view, is minimal contact.

Interaction between former spouses. In spite of these attitudes, some former spouses express feelings of friendship, caring, compassion, and warm feelings for each other. In addition to talking about children, they discuss friends, relatives, new experiences, finances (not related to children), personal problems, and help each other with household tasks. However, they seldom talk about present relationships, why they got divorced, reconciliation, or the possibility of dating each other (Ahrons and Wallisch, 1986; Goldsmith, 1980). This interaction decreases over time, and men, in general, are more willing to interact with their former spouses than are women (Goetting, 1979).

When former spouses were asked how they would like to change their nonparental relationship, some indicated dissatisfaction with their current relationship because of too much interaction, while others reported dissatisfaction because of too little interaction. Specifically, some divorced persons seemed to prefer less interference in their private lives by their former spouses whereas others wished they and their former spouse could be closer, spend more time together, and be friendlier and less antagonistic; a few even expressed the desire to return to predivorce conditions. Others regretted the loss of contact with friends and relatives because of the divorce.

The differences in former spouse relationships is evident in the typology developed by Ahrons and Rodgers (1987):

Perfect pals: These couples enjoyed spending much time together and even shared activities without the children. None of the couples have remarried.

Cooperative colleagues: These couples got along well, but spent less time together and interacted mostly about their children. They have been able to put their anger aside and focus on parental issues. Many have remarried.

Angry associates: These couples only communicated about issues concerning their children and are quick to fight.

Fiery foes: These couples went out of their way to avoid meeting or even talking to each other. They often forced their children to "choose sides."

SUMMARY

Adjusting to a divorce is a long-term process starting long before the legal divorce, and it usually continues long after. It involves almost every facet of one's life: social, emotional, and material. Because of differential sex-role socialization and economic factors, men and women react differently to divorce. While divorce is a positive experience for some people, others experience stress to a degree that may result in both physical and mental health problems, alcoholism, accidents, or even death. Divorce adjustment may involve a short-term reaction that is characterized by a temporary state of personality disorganization or a long-term reaction that culminates in a wide range of outcomes—from psychopathology to strengthened functioning.

One of the major challenges for divorced spouses is to work through their postdivorce relationship. This relationship includes parental and nonparental roles. Some couples fail to do this because they have not resolved the conflicts that characterized their marriage.

REVIEW QUESTIONS

1. Discuss how stress resulting from the divorce process affects people's physical and emotional health.
2. How and why does divorce affect men and women differently?
3. According to Kessler, what are the stages of divorce adjustment that take place after separation?
4. What are several factors related to divorce adjustment and how are these related?
5. What are some of the games divorced people could play with each other?

SUGGESTED PROJECTS

1. Read a popular book about divorce, such as *The Divorce Experience* by Hunt and Hunt, or *Creative Divorce* by Krantzler. How do these authors address stress created by divorce?
2. Write a newspaper column explaining why divorced people continue to play games with each other and how they might be more constructive in their interactions with each other.
3. Collect magazine articles about divorce adjustment. What are the major themes appearing in these articles?

CHAPTER

5

Children and Divorce

The greatest anxiety that Americans show about divorce is about the children of divorced parents. [Lerner, 1957: 597]

SINCE 1900, APPROXIMATELY 25-30% of all children in the United States have experienced marital dissolution, and it is estimated that in the 1980s 40-50% of all children may be affected (Bane, 1976; Glick, 1979). The total number of children involved in divorce has more than tripled over the last two decades (U.S. Bureau of the Census, 1979) to the extent that approximately 60% of all divorcing couples have one or more children at home (Glick, 1979). This is in sharp contrast to the time when the presence of minor children in the home was thought to serve as a major deterrent to divorce.

The rising divorce rate among couples with children has resulted in a corresponding increase in single-parent families. In 1984, approximately one-fifth of all children resided in a single-parent household (with divorced, never married, or widowed parents); this is more than double the number of single-parent households in 1970 (Norton and Glick, 1986). Only 63% of all children reside with both natural parents in a first marriage, and this figure is expected to decline to 56% by 1990. Although the number of children of divorce living with their fathers has tripled since 1970, only 10% of all divorced fathers have primary custody of their children ("One-Fifth of America's Children," 1982; Glick and Norton, 1980).

PERIOD OF SEPARATION

Divorce as Crisis

Divorce is a significant process in the life of a child; it represents a sense of loss, a sense of failure in interpersonal relationships, and the beginning of an often-difficult transition to a new family lifestyle (Magrab, 1978). Children of divorce, however, should not be considered fundamentally different from other children because the majority are healthy, normal children who are confronted with an extremely stressful situation. In fact, it has long been established that children of divorce may be better adjusted than children remaining in two-parent homes where there is on-going tension, conflict, and stress (e.g., Despert, 1962; Landis, 1960; Nye, 1957). Also, divorce is often the most positive solution to destructive family functioning (Hetherington et al., 1978).

In assessing the crisis effect of divorce, it should be noted that the "divorce-related" problems of many children from divorced families are present prior to separation and are related to preexisting family dynamics. Children's emotional responses to both divorce and marital conflict are, in fact, very similar (Moreland et al., 1982). In addition, although prolonged separation of a child from his or her parent is often assumed to be related to serious problems in socioemotional development, the existence of such problems has not been empirically supported. Rather, it is the extent of family discord, not the separation per se, that is related to maladaptive behavior (Rutter, 1971).

Much of the literature on the impact of divorce on children has presented a rather negative picture because of its clinical orientation. Clinical studies focus on children most severely affected by divorce. In addition, these studies have focused on the negative, that is, the problems and failures in coping rather than strengths and coping abilities (Longfellow, 1979; Raschke, 1987).

Major advancements in our understanding of how children are affected by divorce have been made by the recent works of Hetherington et al. (1976, 1978, 1979a, 1979b, 1979c, 1985), Wallerstein and Kelly (1980), and Wallerstein (1984, 1985, 1986). While these works are considered "benchmark" studies by many, some family professionals have questioned their generalizability to larger populations.

The Initial Response

For most children, the news of their parents' divorce is distressing and shocking. However, the degree of distress and shock depends on how parents convey the news. Not surprisingly, many parents, because of their own feelings of emotional instability and fear that their children may reject them or become upset, experience much difficulty in telling their children. In fact, most parents are so anxious and uncomfortable, the result is often a pronouncement with little time devoted to details that are important to children, that is, answering questions children may have or allowing time for the children to express their feelings. Typically, parents gloss over the real reasons for the divorce, and children are not emotionally reassured or told how the divorce will affect them. Consequently, children are often left to contemplate their worst fears. In extreme cases, parents do not tell the children about the divorce because they believe the children could not understand. In these cases, children are left to learn about the divorce from others or indirectly by overhearing adult conversations.

Parents' ability to comfort their children and provide a clear, rational explanation is strongly related to the intensity of the children's reaction and fearfulness (Jacobson, 1978; Wallerstein and Kelly, 1980). Children's coping ability appears to be directly related to viewing the parents' decision as carefully considered, rational, and bringing some happiness or relief to at least one parent (Wallerstein and Kelly, 1980). In addition, several authors (e.g., Anthony, 1974; Whiteside, 1982) have emphasized that without a clear understanding of the divorce, children are less able to move toward the acceptance of a new family structure.

Regardless of how parents inform their children of the impending divorce, children are rarely prepared for the news and are seldom able to accept it. Even if children have lived much of their lives in an unhappy home, they ordinarily do not perceive divorce as a positive solution to family unhappiness (Wallerstein and Kelly, 1980). They usually perceive that their prefamily situation is as good as that of other intact families with which they are familiar. "The divorce is a bolt of lightning that struck them when they had not even been aware of a need to come in from the storm" (Wallerstein, 1980: 67). It would thus appear that if children were asked, there would be no divorce.

Children's initial reaction to the news of their parents' divorce may be characterized by overwhelming feelings of loss. Not only is there a loss of the noncustodial parent, but perhaps the loss of several familiar supports, such as daily routine; the symbols, traditions, and continuity of the intact family; and home, school, and neighborhood. This "loss" perspective or theory, based on the work of Elizabeth Kubler-Ross (1969), has been used as the basis for many intervention programs for parents, teachers, and helping professionals (also see Chapter 8).

Based on the Kubler-Ross (1969) model, Hozman and Froiland (1977) delineated a series of five stages of emotional reaction to the losses that children pass through in the process of adjusting to their parents' separation and divorce.

Stage 1: Denial. During the denial stage, the child chooses not to accept objective reality, but instead perceives the world as she or he would like it to be. For example, the child may withdraw from others into a fantasy world of images of a happy family life prior to divorce.

Stage 2: Anger. During the anger stage, the child frequently attempts to strike out at anyone with whom she or he is involved in hope that negative attention will engage both parents and bring about a reconciliation. For example, the child may direct emotional outbursts toward those who take the place of parents, such as school personnel.

Stage 3: Bargaining. When denial and anger prove to be nonproductive, the child will enter the bargaining stage. The child in essence "makes a deal" with himself or herself to overcome the loss. For example, a child may imagine that improvement in his or her behavior will result in a reconciliation.

Stage 4: Depression. In time, a mourning about the loss begins. When the child discovers that she or he cannot control or have an impact on his or her environment, she or he becomes depressed. For example, the child may regret past "bad" behaviors with a parent and blame himself or herself for the divorce.

Stage 5: Acceptance. Acceptance comes when the child learns that there is an objective reality that exists, whether or not she or he likes it. For example, a child may realize that his or her father will not be available as often as she or he would like, but that a satisfactory relationship will continue to exist with the father, yet in a different form.

Many clinicians view the child's subsequent development as negatively affected if he or she does not experience or "work through" these emotional responses. However, these stages may not occur in a clear, progressive fashion because regression to a prior stage or an overlapping of stages is common.

A wide range of somatic disturbances also appear related to children's reaction to the news of their parents' divorce—overactivity, anorexia, nausea, vomiting, diarrhea, urinary frequency, and sleep disturbances. In addition, for certain groups of children, such as the handicapped, adopted, or children with asthma, epilepsy, and diabetes, the parents' divorce may bring about a crisis demanding medical attention (Anthony, 1974).

Scholars do not agree about the length of time that children experience these intense emotional reactions. For example, in their 5-year follow-up study, Wallerstein and Kelly (1980) found that while 34% of the children were happy and thriving and 29% were doing reasonably well, 37% were still depressed. Stronger indications of the long-term impact of divorce on children were reported by Wallerstein (1984), who found in her 10-year follow-up study that for 30% of the children, divorce had remained a central focal point of their lives and still evoked strong feelings, fear, and profound loneliness. In addition, one-half of her sample still harbored reconciliation fantasies.

In contrast to this long-term impact, Hetherington et al. (1978) found that although most children did not experience any marked reduction in tension or increase in their sense of well-being until one year following the divorce, most children in their study were in a process of restabilization and adjustment within two years of the divorce. In their 6-year follow-up, negative effects of divorce still prevalent were not specifically related to the loss of a parent but were largely attributed to various negative life changes the children had experienced, such as alterations in child care, moves to different locales, and mental and physical problems of family members (Hetherington et al., 1985).

Responses to Divorce

Social scientists have increasingly recognized the wide range of variation in both the quality and the intensity in children's responses to divorce. For example, Hetherington (1979) reported that some children exhibited severe and/or sustained disruptions in development while others seemed to endure a turbulent divorce and stressful aftermath and emerge as competent, well-functioning individuals. Part of this variation could be accounted for by both individual (age, sex, tempera- ment) and situational (previous family relationships, support systems, parenting) factors that influence children's reaction to divorce.

Age. In general, younger children exhibit more severe social and emotional reactions to parental divorce. They also show more anxiety and evidence more somatic complaints, including eating disorders and physical problems (Lowery and Settle, 1985). Wallerstein and Kelly (1980), who conducted a thorough investigation of the relation between age or stage of development and children's reaction to divorce, found that age was the major difference in children's initial responses to divorce. Based on their observations, they were able to differentiate children's reactions by four age groups: preschool children (3-5 years of age); young school-age children (6-8 years of age); older school-age children (9-12 years of age); and adolescents (13-18 years of age). (Children below the age of 3 are thought to have a limited awareness of divorce-related stress.)

Preschool children's self-concepts were particularly affected by parental divorce. This impact is attributed to the children's feeling that the dependability and predictability offered by family relationships was threatened as well as the feeling that the sense of order regarding their world was disrupted. Some of these children suffered feelings of responsibility for "driving" the father away, and often regressed to earlier stages of dependency. Older preschoolers responded better to family turbulence and divorce, often without breaking developmental stride. These children were better able to find gratification outside the home and to place some psychological and social distance between themselves and their parents; however, heightened anxiety and aggression were noted in this group.

The most striking responses among *young school-age children* were pervasive sadness, grief, fear, and deprivation. These children often felt abandoned, wished for the reconciliation of parents, and were characterized by specific fears about their future.

Older school-age children often displayed conscious, intense anger, fears, phobias, and a shaken sense of identity and loneliness. These children also exhibited overt expressions of hostility and anger directed toward the parent they considered most responsible for the divorce.

Adolescents often reacted with feelings of anger, depression, and guilt and these feelings were often related to loyalty conflicts. Withdrawal and distancing from both parents was a common defense. For some adolescents, divorce accelerated the maturation process because they became more realistic, futuristic, and independent than their peers. In contrast, divorce may delay maturation and the resolution of adolescent identity issues (Wallerstein and Kelly, 1980).

Interestingly, in her 10-year follow-up study, Wallerstein (1984) found that, contrary to her earlier findings, younger children were considerably less emotionally burdened than older children. She attributed this finding to the fact that younger children were less able to remember parental conflict or their own fright and suffering at the time of divorce.

The impact of divorce often reaches beyond adolescent children to include young adult children of divorcing/divorced parents. Young adults can be very much affected by parental divorce even if they have left home. They often experience emotional reactions similar to children and adolescents, and their relationship with their parents may be negatively affected for long periods of time ("Young Adult Children," 1986).

Gender. Even though parents are less likely to divorce if they have sons rather than daughters, researchers have reported that the impact of divorce is more traumatic, pervasive, and enduring for boys than for girls (Hess and Camara, 1979; Hetherington et al., 1978; McDermott, 1968; Wallerstein and Kelly, 1980). Several reasons have been offered to account for this difference, including the fact that boys are more often exposed to parental conflict, and that it is the father who usually leaves the parental home, resulting in sons more often losing the same-sex parent (McDermott, 1968; Hetherington, 1979). Also, boys, in general, are more aggressive and less compliant than girls. Therefore, they may present greater discipline and control problems in a mother-headed household in which the father is absent. This finding is supported by additional findings of Hetherington and her colleagues and Wallerstein and Kelly, who found that boys received less positive support and nurturance and were viewed more negatively by mothers, teachers, and peers in the period immediately following the divorce. This negative view of boys could be the result of their being identified with their father, or they could simply be perceived as less emotionally needy than girls.

Temperament. Temperamentally difficult children are less adaptable to change and more vulnerable to adversity than other children. "Difficult" children are more likely to be the elicitors, as well as the targets, of negative responses by parents. In contrast, "easy" children tend to have positive moods and react to new situations with low intensity and are less likely to receive negative parental responses, displaced anger, and anxiety. These "easy" children are better able to cope with the changes related to divorce. This thesis was substantiated by Hetherington and her colleagues (1978) when they found that children who responded most adversely to divorce were described by their mothers as having been difficult infants. Wallerstein and Kelly (1980) also found that children who had histories of maladjustment preceding the divorce were more likely to experience longer-lasting emotional disturbance following the divorce.

Predivorce family relationships. It is generally assumed that it is "difficult to separate the effects of divorce from those of the prolonged trauma and strain preceding it" (McDermott, 1968: 1424). However, several researchers have attempted to investigate those aspects of marital and family relationships prior to parental separation that may have an impact on a child's response to divorce.

In general, children's positive relationship with both parents prior to divorce tends to carry over to the postdivorce family. On the other hand, children are more vulnerable to disengagement by a parent with whom they have been close prior to the divorce. Children's exposure to parental hostility and conflict, including physical violence (which is not uncommon), is related to poor adjustment to the parental divorce (Jacobson, 1978: Kurdek and Siesky, 1980; McDermott, 1970). This is particularly true when the marital conflict focused on issues directly related to the children (Hetherington, 1979).

However, a child's perception of family adjustment and conflict may be more important than the actual amount of family dysfunction exhibited. Many parents are able to conceal their interpersonal conflict and fulfill the roles of effective and nurturant parents. In these cases, children may be shocked to learn of the divorce (Magrab, 1978; Wallerstein and Kelly, 1980). In contrast, children may respond positively to parental divorce if the result is a marked reduction in tension and conflict (Lowery and Settle, 1985).

Parenting during separation. The strength and quality of the parent-child relationship is an important predictor of a child's ability to adjust to parental divorce (Hess and Camara, 1979; Hetherington et al., 1978). However, during the period of separation, parents usually experience a "diminished capacity to parent" (Wallerstein and Kelly, 1980). Hetherington et al. (1978) found that parents' feelings of helplessness interfered with their parenting abilities. Specifically, separated parents, when compared to parents in intact families, were less consistent and effective with discipline, less nurturant, generally behaved less appropriately with their children, communicated less well with their children, and made fewer demands for mature behavior.

Depression characterizes many people during the period of separation. Wallerstein and Kelly (1980) found that parents were often immobilized in their capacity to comfort their children or attend to their children's specific needs. As a result, these children typically experienced a heightened sense of anxiety and concern for the future. Long-term reactions to such parenting may result in what Wallerstein (1985) terms the "overburdened child"—children whose responsibilities for self and others do not allow maintenance of their own developmental course.

During the period of separation, parents are also beginning to cope with the demands of functioning as single parents. For the custodial parent—typically the mother—this often means coping with additional financial difficulties, moving to a new residence, and experiencing "role overload" as a result of her added responsibilities as head of household plus breadwinner. For the noncustodial parent—usually the father—the single-parent status may mean dealing with the loss of a familiar residence, the loss of a meaningful relationship with his children, and the lack of skills needed to run a household. These changes not only impair their roles as effective parents, but also add to the instability with which children of divorce must often deal.

During separation, it is not unusual that parents express high levels of conflict, including physical violence (Hetherington, 1979; Wallerstein and Kelly, 1980). Hetherington found that during the period of separation, approximately two-thirds of the exchanges between spouses involved conflict, and Wallerstein and Kelly described this period as being accompanied by "primitive angers" that may not have been a part of their predivorce style of marital interaction.

During this period, there is often little attempt to shield children from this overt conflict, and some parents seem to want the children as an audience. This conflict not only increases the child's feelings of insecurity, but also places the child in a position of dealing with conflicting loyalties (Hetherington, 1979; Wallerstein and Kelly, 1980).

Support systems. Because of parents' diminished capacity to parent, the availability and accessibility of other support systems becomes paramount for children. This was very evident in Wallerstein and Kelly's study (1980), as over one-half of the children in their study felt their fathers were insensitive to their needs, and one-third felt their mothers were unaware of their distress. Therefore, siblings, friends, and even neighbors become important sources of support for children experiencing divorce. Siblings can be a major source of comfort during this time—either by sharing feelings and reassurance, or merely by symbolizing stability because of their continuing presence. Similarly, peers can help older children detach themselves from the intensity of divorce and serve as confidants with whom to share divorce-related concerns (Hetherington, 1979; Kurdek and Siesky, 1980).

Extended family members are logical sources of support for children experiencing divorce. However, this source of support is often lacking because of the mobility of families (accompanied with a decline in extended family relationships), family members' involvement in their own problems, or the stigma still associated with divorce. Even close family members often limit their support because of the negative attitudes that they hold about divorce (Kitson et al., 1982). Wallerstein and Kelly (1980) found that three-fourths of the children in their study were not helped by grandparents, uncles, or aunts. In contrast, grandparents who did help were viewed as very helpful, and their grandchildren appeared to benefit from their special concern and care.

Support from neighbors, family friends, and other community members appears to be almost completely absent. Wallerstein and Kelly (1980) found fewer than 5% of the children in their sample were counseled or assisted in any way by a church congregation or minister, and less than 10% of the children received adult help from their community or family friends. The exception to this pattern was found in the schools. School was helpful to these children, largely because of its continuing presence in their lives and because it tended to provide much-needed structure and serve as a refuge from family problems. However, for the most part, teachers themselves were not particularly helpful as they were unfamiliar with the children's emotional reactions and needs resulting from the divorce.

SINGLE-PARENT FAMILIES

Divorce for families is often viewed as involving two phases: (a) the crisis of divorce and (b) the development of the single-parent family.

Because approximately one out of every five divorced adults remarries within the first year after divorce and approximately four out of five eventually remarry, many view the single-parent family as a temporary or transitional structure. This family structure is one that the majority of divorcing parents and children will experience for a limited time, but for others it will become a permanent lifestyle (Glick, 1984; Hetherington and Parke, 1979; Ross and Sawhill, 1975).

The transition to living in a single-parent family is usually stressful for both parents and children. This stress may be attributed to the simultaneous adjustment to the loss of family members accompanied by development of new patterns of family interaction and adjusting to a new lifestyle. There is strong evidence to suggest that, in the short run (one to two years after the divorce), divorced persons often experience feelings of distress and unhappiness and generally poor relationships with their children (Hetherington, et al., 1978; Wallerstein and Kelly, 1980).

Problems Experienced by Divorced Mothers

Much of the stress experienced by divorced custodial mothers is the result of insufficient economic resources. This scarcity of funds may be attributed to several reasons: (a) divorce often means dividing a family income that might not have sufficiently supported one household, (b) less than one-half of noncustodial fathers contribute to the support of their children as decreed (U.S. Bureau of the Census, 1983b), and (c) divorced women often lack the education, job skills, or experience to obtain well-paying positions. Divorced mothers, as compared to divorced fathers, are more likely to be unemployed or have low-paying, often part-time jobs, or positions of limited duration. Longfellow (1979) contends that the absence of the father may have its most direct impact not on the child but on the social and economic position of the family. In sum, the parent least able to financially support a couple's children must do so, and may, as a result of lack of resources, turn to her parents or other relatives for financial assistance (see Chapter 7).

Single custodial parents, as a result of having to cope with the needs and tasks ordinarily carried out by two parents, often experience role overload. While it is generally assumed that some children of divorce suffer from paternal deprivation, they may also suffer from maternal deprivation as the divorced mother struggles to meet the demands of household tasks, child care, and economic pressures. Consequently, these families often live a "chaotic lifestyle" because family responsibilities are not well delineated and many routine chores do not get accomplished (Hetherington et al., 1978).

Mothers in single-parent families are often socially isolated, therefore lacking needed social and emotional support. Because of economic pressures, it is not unusual that single-parent families move to more modest housing, thereby losing the support of friends, neighbors, a familiar school, and a community environment. In addition, these new neighborhoods may have higher delinquency rates, greater risks to personal safety, fewer recreational facilities, and inadequate schooling (Hetherington, 1979; Hodges et al., 1979).

Folk wisdom would have us believe that the presence of children would help to ameliorate the divorced mother's feelings of social isolation and loneliness. Actually, research indicates the presence of children may contribute to the mothers' feelings of unhappiness, frustration, helplessness, and incompetency (Bloom and Hodges, 1981; Hetherington et al., 1978). As a result, many divorced mothers feel locked into a world that is filled with never-ending responsibilities of child rearing without sufficient social, emotional, and economic support.

Divorced Fathers

Noncustodial divorced fathers also experience a variety of stressors related to the changes in their family structure. Like their former spouses, noncustodial fathers initially live a chaotic lifestyle as they attempt to maintain a household. During this period, it becomes evident that many divorced men never learned the necessary skills for management of a household, or even how to take care of themselves. Noncustodial fathers, compared to married men, are more likely to rely on carry-out meals, eat at irregular times, and eat away from home. In addition, they sleep less, have more erratic sleep patterns, and have more difficulty with household tasks such as shopping, cooking, laundry, and cleaning (Hetherington et al., 1976).

Divorced fathers who attempt to support two households are often plagued by financial problems. In addition, they may be in continual conflict with former spouses over finances. As a result of increased financial pressure, some divorced fathers are likely to increase their workload; this tendency to work overtime coupled with an inability to work effectively because of emotional problems often increases their stress.

Noncustodial fathers also experience social isolation and loneliness. These men often move from their "home" neighborhood, resulting in a loss of an established support system and contact with friends. In contrast to custodial mothers, who feel trapped, divorced fathers often complain of feeling excluded, rootless, at loose ends, and of a need to engage in social activities—even if not pleasurable. Noncustodial fathers also frequently report intense feelings of isolation that result in their rapidly moving into new relationships (Hetherington et al., 1976).

Conflict Following the Divorce

It is not uncommon for parents to experience postdivorce conflict. It has been noted that divorce alters, but does not end, a spousal relationship, and this is particularly true if children are involved (e.g., Anthony, 1974; Hetherington et al., 1978; Wallerstein and Kelly, 1980; Weiss, 1975). It is ironic that parents who did not get along while married are asked by society to interact in a reasonable and calm manner when divorced. Some divorced parents continue to remain involved with each other only through hostility and conflict (Hetherington et al., 1978; Kressel et al., 1980; Weiss, 1975). For example, in the Hetherington study, two months after the divorce, relationships with the former spouse were characterized as conflictual. The most common areas of conflict included finances and support payments, visitation and child rearing, and intimate relations with others (see Chapter 4).

Custody and visitation patterns are often areas of conflict between former spouses. Wallerstein and Kelly (1979) estimated that 10 to 15% of divorce cases that involve children are litigated over these issues. In addition, Cline and Westman (1971) found one-half of 105 divorce cases involving children were followed by hostile interaction requiring court intervention within two years of the divorce. Children are often used as pawns or mechanisms whereby former spouses can express anger toward each other. Interestingly, fighting may have some beneficial side effects for parents, including the warding off of depression (Wallerstein and Kelly, 1980).

Changes in Parenting

The continuing conflict between divorced parents often results in major disruptions in parenting. Hetherington and her colleagues (1978) found that, in general, divorced parents were (a) more inconsistent in their use of discipline, (b) less affectionate with their children, (c) had greater difficulty controlling their children, (d) had more trouble communicating with their children, and (e) held fewer expectations for mature behavior. Adding to this inconsistency and confusion, they also found major differences between former spouses on child rearing issues.

These changes in parenting were most evident one year after the divorce—particularly for the mothers. For many, the divorce marked the first time they assumed sole responsibility for gaining their children's cooperation and providing discipline. These experiences resulted in the mothers often feeling frightened and inadequate. In addition, their parenting was negatively affected by their children's divorce-related problems; children, particularly sons, became more independent, less compliant, and more angry and aggressive as they adjusted to a new lifestyle (Moreland et al., 1982). Fortunately, Hetherington et al. (1979) found that most families approached a more stable pattern of life two years after the divorce. By this time, divorced mothers were (a) demanding more independent, mature behavior, (b) communicating more effectively (using more explanations and reassurance), (c) were more nurturant and consistent, and (d) were better able to control their children.

A similar pattern of improvement in parenting also was found for noncustodial fathers in terms of maturity demands, communication, and consistency (Hetherington et al., 1976). However, over time, noncustodial fathers became less nurturant and more detached from their children: "Two years after the divorce, divorced fathers clearly are influencing their children less and divorced mothers more" (p. 426).

A pervasive concern of noncustodial fathers is the possibility of losing their children. Many begin to feel they are no longer fathers; they may feel they are not needed by their children, their children belong to their mothers, and/or their authority as a parent has been taken away (Atkin and Rubin, 1976). When married, many fathers rely on their wives to organize and initiate activities and to communicate with their children; as a result, many fathers, after divorce, lack the knowledge of how to interact with their children (Moreland and Schwebel, 1981). Contrary to popular belief, Seagull and Seagull (1977) contend that the temporary presence of the noncustodial father's children does not ease this feeling of loss but, instead, tends to renew the mourning process.

Divorced fathers are often consumed with feelings of incompetency and failure as a parent. These feelings are reinforced by a society that often blames fathers for divorce. In contrast, however, some noncustodial fathers actually experience greater closeness with their children than when married (e.g., Friedman, 1980; Weiss, 1979).

Visitation

For the vast majority of children in divorced families, visitation refers to maintaining contact with the noncustodial father, and this contact is considered crucial for the child's successful adjustment to divorce and subsequent development. Jacobson (1978) found that children who had failed to spend much time with their fathers in the first year after divorce were more likely to develop emotional problems. Wallerstein and Kelly (1980) also reported that childhood depression was related to diminished contact with the father, whereas self-esteem was enhanced by the maintenance and consistency of a strong father-child relationship.

Both noncustodial fathers and children express feelings of dissatisfaction about visitation; only 20% of the children in Wallerstein and Kelly's (1980) study reported that visitation provided enough contact with their fathers. In addition, visitation often heightens feelings of loss and depression in fathers—to the point that some reduce contact with their children because it is too painful (Hetherington et al., 1976). Other fathers find visitation to be so artificial and meaningless that contact is gradually reduced. The result is that noncustodial fathers increasingly socialize with their children from a distance and with a great deal of laxity; they often become pals more than parents (Furstenberg and Nord, 1985).

Wallerstein and Kelly (1980) attempted to determine factors that are predictive of a consistent pattern of father-visitation. Surprisingly, they found the father's predivorce relationship with his children was not necessarily related to the maintenance of a frequent and consistent pattern of visitation. Instead, fathers' initial visitation patterns were determined by their feelings about the divorce, by the age and sex of the children, and by the child's responsiveness. Fathers were more likely to visit younger children (aged 2-8) and sons frequently and consistently; these relationships were viewed as easier to maintain because the children tended to be more responsive. Frequent and consistent visitation patterns were also related to a better postdivorce former spouse relationship. In addition, when a father has responsibility for his children on a frequent basis for long periods of time, as the result of either joint custody or a visitation agreement, he is more likely to view his role as significant and to continue to provide emotional and financial support (Friedman, 1980; Lowery and Settle, 1985).

Visitation with children tends to become more enjoyable for noncustodial fathers one year after the divorce, resulting in a more stable pattern of visitation. In addition, sex differences in visitation patterns diminish and visitation becomes more flexible and responsive to children's needs (Wallerstein and Kelly, 1980). However, in the Wallerstein and Kelly study, 8% of the fathers had ceased all contact within one year after the divorce and others failed to establish any consistent pattern of contact with their children. Similarly, Furstenberg and Nord (1985), in a study of over 200 children of divorce, found fathers' visitations averaged less than two visits per month (the standard visitation period in some states) and that overall contact with the noncustodial parent declined over time; approximately 50% of the children in this study had not seen their nonresident fathers in the past year.

Custody Arrangements

In recent years, fathers have been assuming more nurturant, expressive, and responsible roles with their children. These changes have emerged as women have found additional roles beyond child rearing. As a result, more divorcing fathers now seek primary or joint custody of their children, and more mothers appear to be willing to share custody or give up primary custody.

It is sometimes assumed that a father seeks custody of his children only to hurt his former spouse or because he believes the former spouse is an unfit parent. Yet research suggests that most fathers seek custody because of love and concern for their children, along with a sense of confidence in their parenting ability. (However, a significant minority use the threat of primary or joint custody, when they do not actually want it, as leverage to obtain a lower child support assessment or some other economic advantage in the settlement agreement.) The father who is most likely to seek custody tends to be more highly educated and financially secure, and his children are older and more often boys; boys are often viewed as more difficult to rear and, therefore, may relate better to their father, especially at older ages (Norton and Glick, 1986).

Despite some minor difficulties, most custodial fathers report satisfactory adjustment to having sole responsibility for their children. Risman (1986), in a recent study of 141 single fathers, found that most men felt comfortable and competent as single parents, regardless of the reason for custody or their financial status. This is not to say that paternal custody is problem-free; custodial fathers do report having problems in supervising their children, meeting the children's emotional needs, carrying out homemaking tasks, and meeting the special needs of daughters (Mendes, 1976). Like custodial mothers, they exhibit conflict over reconciling parental and adult roles, finding time to spend with children, and problems making decisions alone (Orthner et al., 1976).

Some professionals (e.g., Santrock and Warshak, 1979) have stressed the importance of maximum contact with the same-sex parent and have questioned custody arrangements (that is, father or mother) where contact with the same-sex parent was minimized. These authors contend that a child of the opposite sex may represent a substitute for the absent spouse, and this arrangement may lead to an unhealthy relationship. However, the majority of researchers contend that the economic status and social-psychological adjustment of the custodial parent are far more important factors than the parent's sex in contributing to a positive child-custody arrangement.

Joint custody, even though highly controversial among both legal and mental health professionals, is an increasingly popular alternative designed to facilitate the child's postdivorce relationship with both parents and acknowledge the parental rights of both mother and father. Joint legal custody can be defined as a situation where parents share decision-making authority and child rearing responsibility after divorce; if the children also reside in both parents' households, then it is termed joint physical custody. The primary concern of professionals centers on cases of joint physical custody; they fear that these children might be forced to live in two discontinuous and unsettled environments and be prevented from forming a strong emotional relationship with either parent. However, studies (e.g., Abarbanel, 1979; Steinman, 1981) that have evaluated joint physical custody have arrived at similar conclusions—parents are generally satisfied and children are well adjusted. One study that compared joint to sole custody (Luepnitz, 1982) concluded that joint physical custody had more advantages and fewer disadvantages. Joint-custody parents had better relationships with each other, were more likely to honor child support agreements, experienced less geographic mobility, and felt less overwhelmed by child care responsibilities than sole-custody parents. The success of this arrangement, however, is contingent on parental cooperation, flexibility, mutual support, and respect. Steinman (1981) concluded that joint custody is not beneficial for all divorced families. It may, in fact, be harmful if (a) it increases the role of the child in parental conflict, (b) it interferes with school attendance, and (c) it confuses a child by constant shuttling between two homes (Gardner, 1982).

Split-custody is a rare custodial arrangement that involves dividing siblings, that is, placing one or more in the custody of each parent. While little is known about the results of such an arrangement, both parents and the courts view it with disfavor (Lowery and Settle, 1985).

Impact of the Single-Parent Family Structure on Child Development

As previously mentioned, when a family unit becomes two single-parent units, effective parenting is often disrupted. These changes in parental effectiveness can have short-term as well as long-term effects on children. Children's developmental needs do not subside or change as a result of changes in family structure, and it appears that single-parent families, compared to two-parent families, may be less adaptive economically, socially, and psychologically (Wallerstein and Kelly,

1980). This is not to say that single parents cannot provide the necessary nurturance required for the successful development of a child, but that the psychological stress, economic problems, and the absence of the supporting presence of another parent make it more difficult.

Research that has investigated the long-term impact of single-parenting on children (for example, Hetherington et al., 1978; Jones, 1977; Kurdek et al., 1981) has concluded that most acute symptoms that are reactions to divorce tend to diminish within two years, and most children resume their normal developmental progress. A few authors maintain that the divorce experience can be related to long-term social and psychological problems, including conduct disorders, impaired intellectual and academic functioning, social interaction difficulties, and problems in sex-role development. However, most also suggest that long-term problems appear to be more related to problems experienced by single-parent families than the divorce experience or resulting father absence. In general, most of the long-term problems experienced by children of divorce are the products of poverty and disruption in lifestyle and the conflictual nature of the relationship between parents prior to and following the divorce (Herzog and Sudia, 1971; Raschke and Raschke, 1979). Poverty, however, is commonly viewed as having the greatest impact on children of divorce, as it affects stress levels, support systems, and quality of housing, and is often related to changes in neighborhoods, peer groups, and schools.

Many of the long-term negative effects of divorce can be mitigated if the child maintains positive relationships with both parents and if the parents are cooperative (Esman, 1971). Such relationships also tend to be characterized by greater economic support of the child. Kurdek and his colleagues (1981) found that close proximity to the noncustodial parent, low parental conflict and hostility, and high agreement between parents on child rearing issues were largely related to the child's ultimate adjustment. However, such cooperation is often lacking. Furstenberg and Nord (1985) found little communication about the children between former spouses. It should, however, be noted that a child's good relationship with one parent often serves as a buffer against a poor relationship with the other (Hess and Camara, 1979).

SUMMARY

The number of children involved in divorce has continued to increase in recent years even though the divorce rate has stabilized. Divorce is typically a very painful experience for children as a result of the many changes and losses experienced in the process. While some researchers conclude that a child ordinarily adjusts to divorce within two years after the divorce, others indicate some long-term reactions, extending into adulthood in some cases. A child's reaction to divorce is mediated by a variety of factors, including the child's sex, age, and temperament; the quality of family relationships prior to and after the divorce; ability of parents to assume the single-parent role; extent and availability of support systems; and opportunity for a meaningful relationship with the noncustodial parent.

Mothers and fathers typically demonstrate diminished parenting ability as they adjust to divorce. This change in parenting is often related to emotional distress, social isolation and loneliness, economic problems, role overload, and continuing conflict with the former spouse. Yet, in the long run, most single parents successfully adapt to the single-parent family structure. Variations in parental custody arrangements are increasingly evident and reflect the more egalitarian nature of mother and father roles; preliminary research findings indicate that primary custody by fathers and joint custody are viable custodial arrangements for many parents and children.

REVIEW QUESTIONS

1. Identify the living arrangements of children today in the U.S., according to type of parental household.
2. Describe the stages that children typically pass through as they adjust to divorce.
3. What factors appear to affect how a child will react to parental divorce?
4. Describe how a child's lifestyle is likely to change after divorce.
5. What particular problems do (a) mothers and (b) fathers experience after divorce that affect their parenting abilities?
6. What are the advantages and disadvantages of joint custody?
7. What are the long-term consequences of divorce on a child's subsequent development?

SUGGESTED PROJECTS

1. Develop a bibliography of materials (for example, books, articles, films) to help parents and children understand the impact of divorce on children.
2. Interview a classroom teacher to find out what problems she or he sees in children experiencing divorce and how she or he handles these situations.
3. Review some studies of children in stepfamilies. Assess the advantages and disadvantages of this family structure for children of divorce.
4. Attend a Parents Without Partners meeting and talk to people about how their children have adjusted or are adjusting to divorce.

CHAPTER

6

Legal Aspects of Divorce

[It was assumed under traditional divorce law] that marital happiness is best secured by making marriage indissoluble except for a very few causes. When the parties know that they are bound together for life, the argument runs, they will resolve their differences and disagreements and make an effort to get along with each other. If they are able to separate legally upon less serious grounds, they will make no such effort . [Clark, 1968; cited in Weitzman, 1985]

HISTORICAL CONTEXT OF DIVORCE LEGISLATION

Current divorce legislation can be traced back hundreds of years to ecclesiastical times, when marriage and divorce came under the jurisdiction of the church and ecclesiastical courts (Elkin, 1982). At that time, marriage was viewed as a sacrament that could not be resolved by mere mortals. Women and children had no legal rights because they were viewed as property of their husbands and/or fathers. These early Christians also instituted the notions of guilt and fault that still characterize divorce laws today. Church law later became fourteenth-century English common law, which, in turn, became the foundation of United States law.

Marriage under English common law was the merger of husband and wife into a single entity. In reality, even though husband and wife were defined as one, *the one* was the husband (Weitzman, 1981). Under the doctrine of coverture, a woman, when married, lost control and ownership of all property. If she earned an income, her husband was entitled to her wages as part of his estate. Because marriage was "for better or for worse," and "until death do us part," the husband's obligation to his wife was to provide lifelong maintenance and support;

thus it was reasoned that she had no need or use for her own property. If a husband and wife were to separate, the husband had the right to full custody of the couple's children, along with any other "property"; there were no specified visiting rights for the mother. The wife/mother was, in essence, liquidated as a bad investment that did not return expected profits. The English tradition was that the father was the "natural" guardian and educator of the children. Child care was perceived as primarily child training, and fathers were presumed to have superior expertise for this vocationally oriented relationship (Derdeyn, 1976; Weitzman, 1981). (Also see Chapter 7.)

This patriarchal legacy was carried to the American colonies. America thus inherited a divorce tradition that rested on the subordination of married women, a guilt-innocence approach to divorce, and strong antidivorce legislation. Consequently, the same oppressive forces represented in English marriage and divorce laws were instilled in early American law and persist to some degree today (Elkin, 1982).

Fundamental change in American divorce laws did not occur until the nineteenth century, when the Industrial Revolution changed the family structure by moving the center of economic productivity outside the home. The father then became an "absentee" parent, leaving the care and nurturance of his children to his wife as he entered the industrial labor force. The goals of family living, and specifically the rearing of the children, had also changed at this time. Society began to recognize and honor the special experience of childhood. Family life began to be viewed as a formative experience for building character and for consciously and deliberately forming the child from birth to adulthood. If the children were in some sense sacred, then motherhood was nothing less than a holy office. Women achieved a new sense of importance and dignity in meeting their children's needs for nurturance and education (Derdeyn, 1976; Lasch, 1973). The church still maintained control over marriage and divorce, permitting divorce only when one spouse was found to have committed some grave offense against the other, as specified by law. Then the nonoffending or innocent spouse, usually the wife, was granted custody of the children, and she was also granted economic support, since it was assumed she would not be contributing to the support of her household.

Women have until recently continued to be viewed as the "natural" caretakers of children. In general, judges have held that it is in the best interests of children of "tender years" (under school age) not to be separated from their mother unless the mother is "unfit." During the early twentieth century, the idealization of the mother role was strengthened by Freudian psychology, with its emphasis on the importance of the mother-child bond. In 1924, the courts for the first time placed children's rights over those of parents (especially mothers) by formulating the "best interests of the child" doctrine (Oakland, 1984). This opened up the possibility that other responsible adults, including fathers, could become the child's guardian. Today, judges exercise relative freedom in custody decisions because many changes have influenced traditional assumptions, including questioning of the tender years doctrine, increasing concern about sex discrimination, and the deemphasis on fault in child custody decisions (Derdeyn, 1976).

ADVERSARY SYSTEM

Divorce laws changed very little over the course of the twentieth century until the 1970s. Contemporary divorce law is usually thought of in terms of two periods—pre-1970 (adversarial) and post-1970 (no-fault) (Leslie and Korman, 1985). Prior to 1970, the only way that one could obtain a divorce was to publicly prove one's spouse guilty of some legally recognized offense or "grounds" for divorce. The implication was that there was one guilty party and one innocent party in every divorce. This implication changed in 1970, when California's Family Law Act, including no-fault legislation, went into effect. Since that date, all states have enacted some form of no-fault divorce legislation.

Because divorce laws are state laws, there has been much variation in the range and definition of grounds for divorce. For example, until 1966, the state of New York had only one legally acceptable reason for divorce—adultery; in contrast, some states had as many as 20 grounds for divorce. In the pre-1970 period, these grounds for divorce usually consisted of serious offenses because of the difficulty of dissolving a marital union. These grounds for divorce included such offenses as adultery, bigamy, cruelty, conviction of a felony, insanity, nonsupport, and habitual drunkenness. Because of the seriousness of the grounds, women usually brought suit, since it was easier for them to prove fault; it was also considered more chivalrous for men to take the blame. Women were generally viewed by the courts and society as the "wronged" and innocent parties. When alimony was awarded, it was often viewed as punishment of a wrong-doing husband. (The range of grounds used for divorce in the United States today are presented in Table 6.1.)

This adversarial approach maintained the historical legacy of viewing divorce as a necessary evil. Courts prior to 1970 were often interested in making divorce as difficult to secure as possible, believing that this would force couples to resolve their marital differences. This system, however, tended to increase bitterness and hostility between spouses who did divorce and further deteriorated their relationship after the divorce. Judges were trained to find fault, guilt, or breach of agreement

TABLE 6.1
Grounds for Divorce in the United States

	A — Irreconcilable Differences or Irretrievable Breakdown Sole Ground	B — Irreconcilable Differences or Breakdown Added to Traditional Grounds	C — Incompatibility as Grounds	D — Living Separately and Apart as Grounds	E — Judicial Separation or Maintenance as Grounds	F — Mutual Consent Divorce
Alabama		X	X	2 years		
Alaska			X			
Arizona	X					
Arkansas				3 years		X
California	X					X
Colorado	X					X
Connecticut		X		18 months[a]		
Delaware		X	X	6 months		
Florida	X					X
Georgia		X				
Hawaii	X			2 years	any period	X
Idaho		X[b]		5 years		X[b]
Illinois		X[b]		X[b]		
Indiana		X				
Iowa	X					
Kansas			X			
Kentucky	X					
Louisiana				1 year		

State					
Maine		X			
Maryland				1 year[c]	
Massachusetts		X[d]			
Michigan	X				
Minnesota	X				
Mississippi		X			
Missouri		X		1 year[e]	
Montana	X			180 days	
Nebraska	X				
Nevada			X	1 year	
New Hampshire		X			
New Jersey				1½ years	
New Mexico		X			
New York					1 year
North Carolina				1 year	
North Dakota		X			
Ohio			X	1 year	
Oklahoma			X		
Oregon	X				
Pennsylvania		X		3 years[f]	
Rhode Island		X		3 years	
South Carolina				1 year	
South Dakota		X			
Tennessee		X		3 years	
Texas		X		3 years	
Utah				3 years	

Continued

TABLE 6.1 Continued

	A Irreconcilable Differences or Irretrievable Breakdown Sole Ground	B Irreconcilable Differences or Breakdown Added to Traditional Grounds	C Incompatibility as Grounds	D Living Separately and Apart as Grounds	E Judicial Separation or Maintenance as Grounds	F Mutual Consent Divorce
Vermont				6 months		
Virginia				1 year[f]		
Washington	X					X
West Virginia		X		1 year		
Wisconsin	X	X		1 year		
Wyoming						
Washington, D.C.				6 months[g]		
Puerto Rico				2 years		
Virgin Islands	X					

SOURCE: Freed and Walker (1986). Reprinted, with permission, from Family Law Quarterly, Vol. 20, No. 4, Winter 1987. Copyright © 1987 American Bar Association.

a. Eighteen months living separate and apart *and* incompatibility.

b. Irretrievable breakdown *and* two years living separate and apart required; if both parties consent, the period becomes six months.

c. Voluntary twelve consecutive months or two-year uninterrupted separation.

d. Separation agreement also required.

e. One year by mutual consent or two years living separate and apart.

f. Separate and apart for one year is sufficient, six months if there is a separation agreement and there are no children.

g. Six months by voluntary separation, one year living separate and apart.

and then systematically and rationally assess damages, penalties, or sentences (Elkin, 1982).

Actual legal practice during this era, however, usually reflected the reality that marital breakdown arises from "faults" by both spouses. Attorneys often "played with the law" to more expediently, if not more humanely, dissolve a marriage. They typically advised their clients to use the easiest and least embarrassing grounds; these grounds did not necessarily reflect why the couple wanted the divorce (e.g., "cruelty" instead of "adultery"). Even though it was illegal to divorce by mutual consent, most divorce cases did involve some "collusion" or negotiation by the opposing parties prior to going to court and formally placing charges. Approximately 85% of divorce cases prior to 1970 were uncontested and worked out between both spouses and their attorneys prior to going to court. The defendant spouse often did not appear in court and was then judged guilty by default. Rarely did a spouse countercharge if he or she wanted the divorce, since a judge could then deny the divorce (Leslie and Korman, 1985).

Only recently has the judiciary begun to deal with the complexities of the family system by recognizing fault in both parties and facilitating settlements that attempt to provide for the continuing welfare of all family members. However, individuals may still find themselves dealing with aspects of the adversarial approach to divorce. For example, attorneys by nature of their training think adversarily, and often empathize with their client's need for self-vindication and retaliation. Judges, too, because of training and past experience, still feel it necessary to bring out issues of fault and blame before rendering a decision; child custody and visitation decisions, in particular, are still decided by fault to some extent, regardless of the dictates of the law. In addition, if a couple who seeks divorce cannot decide on the terms of a settlement agreement prior to going to court; then, in some states, the traditional adversarial approach must be used.

NO-FAULT DIVORCE PURPOSE

In contrast to the adversarial approach to divorce, no-fault legislation maintains that marriages should be terminated without any imputation of guilt or wrongdoing on the part of either spouse when the marriages are considered no longer viable. Grounds used for divorce include such terms as "irreconcilable differences," "irretrievably broken marriages," "no reasonable likelihood of preserving the marriage," or "dissolution"— concepts not laden with individual blame or fault. As Wheeler (1974) notes:

It is no longer necessary to point the finger of fault at one spouse or the other, so either can start a proceeding to dissolve the marriage. Thus a man or a woman who is having an affair can initiate a divorce, while under traditional notions of law, he or she would be considered "at fault," and thus be barred from doing so. [pp. 20-22]

No-fault legislation has changed four major components of traditional divorce law (Weitzman and Dixon, 1980; Dixon and Weitzman, 1980):

(1) It has eliminated the idea of fault-based grounds for divorce. No one is accused or judged guilty of any offense. The marriage is merely declared unworkable due to undescribed irreconcilable differences and then is dissolved. The individual is empowered to decide when a divorce is justified, that is, one spouse can obtain a divorce without the consent of the other.
(2) It has greatly reduced use of the formal adversary process. It assumes that the adversarial legal process generates hostility and trauma by forcing husbands and wives to be antagonists.
(3) It has based division of financial assets on equity, equality, and economic need rather than fault or sex-role assignments. Financial rewards are not tied to innocence, and it is not assumed that women need to be supported by men. Community property is equally divided under the assumption that both partners have contributed equally, if differently, to the marital partnership. Child custody is based on the sex-neutral principle of the "best interests of the child" rather than maternal preference.
(4) It has redefined the traditional responsibilities of husbands and wives by instituting a new norm of equality between the sexes. The husband and wife are regarded as equal partners, equally responsible for the support of the household and care of the children. Provision of alimony is based on the assumption that the wife will be employed.

Obviously, obtaining a no-fault divorce is usually simpler than going through adversarial procedures. For example, couples often share one attorney or do not even use an attorney if they can work together and formally agree on the issues of division of property, child support, child custody and visitation, and provision of alimony. In California and some other states, "do it yourself" divorce kits are very popular. However, Dixon and Weitzman (1980) caution that couples should be aware that the ease of no-fault procedures is highly related to the number and magnitude of the issues to be resolved and the divorcing couple's ability to compromise, that is, no fault divorce can best expedite the divorce if there are no minor children, no requests for alimony or child support, and no disagreements over property. Marital misconduct may be introduced when child custody, visitation, and alimony are determined. In addition, some states may require counseling, especially if children are involved, and separation periods—both of which may make the no-fault procedures a longer process than the traditional adversarial approach.

Impact of No-Fault Legislation

There was much speculation in the 1970s about possible negative consequences that would ensue for individuals, families, and society if couples could freely dissolve their marriage whenever they chose. Research on short- and long-term effects of no-fault legislation has indicated that such concerns were unwarranted.

Dixon and Weitzman (1980) reviewed court records in Los Angeles and San Francisco in the 1970s in order to assess the impact of California's no-fault divorce legislation. Although they found an increased divorce rate after the introduction of no-fault measures, this increase paralleled the overall increasing divorce rate in the United States at that time. They also pointed out that many individuals prior to 1970 probably postponed their divorce in anticipation of the simpler, less expensive, and less confrontive no-fault divorce, making the divorce rates immediately after the implementation of no-fault appear spuriously high. In addition, shortened residency requirements and waiting periods meant fewer migratory divorces and thus more California divorces. These explanations are similar to those offered by Wright and Stetson (1978) who found no increase in divorce rates, except in California and Florida, as a result of no-fault legislation. Other studies, including Spanier and Casto (1979) and Welch and Price-Bonham (1983), also found no-fault legislation to be unrelated to increasing divorce rates, and, conversely, adversarial approaches unrelated to deterring divorce. Cherlin (1981) concludes that "the spread of no-fault divorce laws seems to have been a reaction to changing attitudes and to the increase in divorce, not a stimulus to more divorce" (p. 49).

In contrast to the fears of some doomsayers who contended no-fault divorce would be the downfall of the American family, Dixon and Weitzman (1980) found that no-fault legislation neither resulted in more impulsive divorces early in marriage nor mothers failing to obtain primary custody of their children. They did find, as anticipated, a sharp drop in litigious actions, a decline in the use of attorneys, and a decline in the frequency and duration of alimony payments. One unanticipated consequence of no-fault divorce is that its gender-neutral rules have placed older homemakers and mothers of young children at economic disadvantage. (For discussion of the economic impact of no-fault divorce, see Chapter 7.)

Interestingly, Dixon and Weitzman (1980) did find that husbands filed for divorce more often after the implementation of no-fault legislation. They concluded that this was because wives no longer had to prove themselves the injured party to receive alimony or one-half the couple's property. Gunter and Johnson (1978) also found a filing role-reversal related to no-fault procedures; they found more males than females filing for divorce in a no-fault county and just the opposite pattern in an adversarial county. They argued that by removing the legal and social stigma attached to divorce, men's chivalry was not questioned by initiation of divorce. It should also be noted that previous grounds, such as cruelty, criminal behaviors, and extramarital sex, were primarily male activities, and were far more easily brought against men by women. Today's grounds under no-fault are neither sex-linked nor denote individual blame (Gunter, 1977).

CHILD CUSTODY

Maternal Preference

It is the responsibility of the court to determine child custody. Typically, however, parents' wishes are honored if they can agree on custody-visitation arrangements (Oakland, 1984). In fact, less than 10% of divorcing parents fail to reach an agreement before the divorce hearing (Weiss, 1979). In these cases, even though all but three states have sex-neutral laws governing custody decisions, courts still favor the mother approximately 90% of the time (McCubbin and Dahl, 1985). This so-called "maternal preference" or tender-years doctrine is based on traditional assumptions concerning parenting (Leslie and Leslie, 1980):

(1) children need mothers more than fathers
(2) mothers are more concerned with child rearing than fathers
(3) the necessity of earning a living interferes with a father's parenting ability

In recent years, as the legal system has responded to sex-role changes and new theories of parenting, there has been a decline in the traditional presumption favoring mothers (Fain, 1977). Historically, a father received custody of his children only if he could convince the court that the children's mother was morally unfit or emotionally unstable. Today, in contrast, more fathers are gaining custody because (a) they have a genuine interest in being the primary caretaker of their children, and (b) mothers are more willing to give them custody of their children (Halem, 1982). The chances of fathers gaining custody of their children are enhanced if their children are older, if the children are sons, and if the father is slightly older and from a higher socioeconomic class (Halem, 1982; Weitzman and Dixon, 1979).

Some authors argue that more fathers could have primary custody if they so desired. This argument is based on the fact that when fathers do seek custody, they obtain custody in about 50% of the cases (McCubbin and Dahl, 1985). Some of the reasons put forth to account for fathers not seeking primary custody include the following:

(1) fathers fear a bitter court battle and the subsequent possibility of having a poor relationship with their children and former spouses

(2) fathers see it as unchivalrous, if not unmanly, to attack the character of their wife and to seek to carry out what society has defined largely as a female role, that is, child rearing

(3) many fathers merely do not want what they perceive as the burdensome responsibility of having primary responsibility for child rearing

(4) many mothers fervently seek primary custody to enhance their general financial settlement and/or to avoid social stigma when, in fact, they might be very satisfied with their former husband's having primary custody

(5) the Equal Rights for Fathers Organization contends there is a "quiet conspiracy" among judges, probation departments, conciliation courts, and even fathers' attorneys to dissuade divorced men from seeking custody (Weitzman, 1981)

(6) courts still base custody decisions to some extent on fault, and it is easier to prove the father at fault and thus a less able parent than the mother

Custody Alternatives

As mentioned in Chapter 5, there are three basic forms of child custody—sole custody, split custody, and joint custody—with many variations, as states have the right to formulate their own custody guidelines. Oakland (1984) has clearly delineated the three types in his book, *Divorced Fathers:*

Sole custody, also referred to as "primary custody," is the preferred arrangement in most states. Sole custody gives one parent full parental authority. The noncustodial parent has no legal right to make any decisions concerning the child, although he or she may have financial obligations to the custodial parent and children. The noncustodial parent is usually awarded legal visitation rights. The schedule for such visits may be set by the court or the two parents.

Sole custody is recognized as having advantages for both parents and children. For parents, it may reduce postdivorce conflict because it minimizes parental interaction/consultation over matters related to children. For children, it is felt that sole custody removes the children from the center of family conflict, and some contend that children have a greater sense of security living in one home, in one neighborhood, and with one set of friends, clothes, toys, and so forth. There are also some recognized disadvantages with sole custody. Noncustodial parents tend to withdraw from their children's lives and this has many negative effects on children, including loss of accustomed intimacy, loss of a role model of a particular sex, and a feeling of abandonment. Some fathers cease child support payments as a part of this withdrawal, resulting in an increasing child rearing burden on the custodial parent.

Split custody. Although rarely used, when a couple has more than one child, they may wish to divide the children, each parent maintaining sole custody of one or more. The most common practice in this pattern is for the boys to go with the father and the girls with the mother. Each custodial parent maintains all parental rights and obligations for the child living with him or her and acts as a noncustodial parent toward the children living with the former spouse.

While split custody is not encouraged by the courts, it does appear to offer some advantages to parents and children. Like sole custody, it eliminates some of the postdivorce conflict that centers around the children, and provides children with stable surroundings. When there are many children, it could ease the child rearing burden of each parent.

There are usually strong reasons for this custody arrangement, including a special bond between one parent and a child, recognition of a child's preference, and the belief that a child will develop a stronger sexual identity by living with a parent of the same sex. Oakland (1984) notes, however, that most of the advantages of split custody accrue to the parents—not to the children. Children lose the support of siblings and may fear rejection by the noncustodial parent. Research findings suggest that judges, parents, and children see the arrangement as basically unsatisfactory, but the best arrangement that could be made.

Joint custody. In 33 states, joint custody is either permitted or given priority when "in the best interests of the child" (Freed and Walker, 1986). Four types of joint custody statutes have been identified (Flynn, 1987; Weitzman, 1985):

(1) *Joint custody as an option.* These laws allow courts to consider equally joint custody along with other custody alternatives.
(2) *Joint custody when parents agree.* This type of statute permits the court to order joint custody only when requested by both parents.
(3) *Joint custody at one party's request.* Under this form of legislation, courts may award joint custody when only one parent has asked for it.

(4) *Joint custody preference or presumption.* A joint custody preference statute requires judges to consider joint custody not as an equal option, but as the preferred custody arrangement. A joint custody presumption indicates that joint custody is in the child's best interests. In order to overcome this presumption, the party who does not want joint custody has to prove that joint custody would be detrimental to the child.

As noted in Chapter 5, there are two forms of joint custody: joint legal custody and joint physical custody. Joint legal custody recognizes the rights of both parents to make major decisions affecting their child's life. Under joint legal custody, physical custody is typically awarded to the mother. Joint legal custody thus closely resembles sole or primary maternal custody with liberal visitation for the father. The increase in joint custody awards can be largely attributed to an increase in awards of joint legal custody. Under joint physical custody, parents share both decision-making responsibilities for and physical care of their child. Although the division of responsibilities may not be equal, the child lives alternately for major periods of time with each parent (Flynn, 1987).

The growing popularity of this form of custody is related to the increased involvement of fathers as parents and of mothers as full-time members of the labor force. Many critics contend that joint custody is also an increasingly popular alternative because it offers an easy way out for courts who dislike the complexity that surrounds such decisions. In an increasing number of jurisdictions, joint custody is now court-imposed, yet many professionals contend that parent commitment and cooperation are essential for this custodial arrangement to work.

The advantages of this arrangement include the opinion of many professionals that joint custody of two caring and committed parents can minimize postdivorce trauma for children. Other advocates suggest that joint custody leads to an improved relationship between former spouses. When physical custody is shared, this arrangement also holds the potential of alleviating the burden of child care faced by the custodial parent.

This arrangement may also be problematic:

(1) two separate authority figures may present loyalty conflicts for a child
(2) the child may feel torn between the values and lifestyles of two "separate" parents
(3) the mere shifting of households in cases of joint physical custody may be confusing to a child
(4) it may be unrealistic to assume that two parents who divorce will be cooperative parents

Legal Rights of Children

Increasingly, courts are paying attention to children's needs and interests in deciding custody. In many states, older children have the right to submit a statement of preference for the court's consideration. The Uniform Marriage and Divorce Act (1970) gives judges discretionary powers to systematically determine the best interests of the child in contested child custody proceedings. Such powers include:

(1) the right to interview children separately in their chambers
(2) the right to appoint *guardians ad litem* to legally represent the interests of children in court
(3) the right to call upon domestic relations investigators or other mental health professionals for assistance

Yet, in most cases, such powers are not exercised. Judges prefer to stay as far removed from these complex and emotional decisions as possible, allowing parents and their attorneys to make these decisions. Also, courts have had to face some conservative groups who fear that the use of these judicial powers in child custody decisions will erode parental rights and undermine the family structure. In the same vein, courts are increasingly granting visitation to extended family members. For example, 42 states now allow grandparents to seek visitation if denied by the custodial parent, and some states are also granting visitation rights to siblings, aunts, and uncles ("For divorce, a revolution in the courtroom," 1983; McCubbin and Dahl, 1985).

Child Stealing

Unfortunately, not all parents are satisfied with the custody arrangements decided by the court. A sizable number of these parents are literally taking the law into their own hands by abducting their child in violation of court orders. Gelles (1984) estimates that between 459,000 and 751,000 incidents of parental child stealing or child snatching occur each year. Fathers (71%) are usually the offenders, reflecting the fact that fathers are less likely to receive sole or primary custody or are denied desired level of contact with their children. The offending parent typically feels a sense of failure and frustration as a result of the loss of the parenting role. For other offenders, the child stealing represents a pathological means for reestablishing the marital relationship (Agopian, 1981).

Abducting parents have also been motivated by certain incongruities in the legal system, primarily the fact that states, until recently, have not had to honor another state's custody decree. Thus a parent could steal his or her child away from the custodial parent and move to another state, where the parent could reopen custody hearings. The Uniform Child Custody Jurisdiction Act (1968) was enacted to prohibit such "forum shopping" or moving children to a new state in hopes of getting a more favorable custody ruling. The reciprocity of enforcement of state custody rulings was accepted by 48 states at that time. This law ensured that only one court has jurisdiction over the child. Yet there was no method to verify another state's prior custody decision, and this law did not provide for the return of the child to the custodial parent, even if the abducting parent made an attempt to seek custody in a new location. The law also did not help if the abducting parent did not try to obtain another custodial decision or if the child was abducted prior to the custody decision, since technically this was not illegal.

The Parental Kidnapping Prevention Act was enacted in 1981 to overcome some of the weaknesses of this 1968 act. This act (1) compels all states to recognize the custody decisions of all other states, (2) authorizes the use of Federal Parent Location Services (originally designed to trace those who default on support payments), and (3) declares that the abductor be treated as an interstate felon, allowing FBI intervention. Certain weaknesses of this law include lack of state cooperation and the law's perspective that "family matters" are not criminal in the traditional sense, thereby making the law less effective than it would appear to be.

SUMMARY

Current divorce legislation is rooted in fourteenth-century common law with its emphasis on marriage as a sacred, lifelong, and patriarchal institution. Divorce legislation in the United States is usually divided into two periods: pre-1970 (adversarial) and post-1970 (no-fault). The adversarial era was characterized by "fault finding" whereby one "innocent" spouse was forced to publicly charge a spouse with a legally recognized offense in order to obtain a divorce and a favorable settlement. The no-fault era represented a move toward a more humane and less punitive method of obtaining a divorce. No-fault has resulted in settlement agreements based more on need and equality than guilt or gender. Contrary to many predictions, no-fault has not resulted in a significant increase in divorce rates, impulsive marriages, nor mothers failing to obtain primary custody of their children. Although many fathers seek out a greater role in child custody, mothers still receive primary custody of their children in about 90% of divorce cases. Joint custody is an increasingly popular custody arrangement, yet it is not appropriate for all divorcing parents and children. Child stealing or snatching has become a pervasive negative effect of parents' dissatisfaction with custody awards in recent years.

REVIEW QUESTIONS

1. Identify the major components of the adversarial approach to divorce. Trace the origin of these ideas.
2. What have been some of the positive and negative effects of no-fault legislation? What could be done to overcome these negative outcomes?
3. How have changing sex roles in American society affected divorce legislation in recent years?
4. What factors are typically considered in (1) division of property, (2) awarding of alimony, (3) child custody, and (4) awarding of child support?
5. Compare and contrast the advantages and disadvantages of the three major custody arrangements for parents, as well as for children. How has joint custody been misused?
6. Why do far more mothers than fathers receive primary custody of their children upon divorce?

SUGGESTED PROJECTS

1. Visit a domestic relations court and observe a divorce case involving child custody.
2. Locate a layperson's legal guide to divorce for your state. Identify significant features that individuals should consider in deciding on and/or initiating divorce.
3. Develop a timeline noting significant factors in the evolution of current divorce legislation in the United States.
4. Read a divorce-related child stealing case in the media and identify factors that prompted this action and what might have been done to have prevented it from happening.
5. Interview a divorce attorney regarding his or her experiences with custody problems.

CHAPTER

7

Economics of Divorce

Four years ago, when I got divorced, my husband and I quickly agreed on financial arrangements. He was angry and seemed to want to punish me. I felt guilty that the marriage had failed, and wanted to soothe his anger. With such closely matched goals, it was easy enough to agree on terms.

Technically, of course, we merely did the modern thing: We split everything down the middle. Everything, that is, except what could be the single most lucrative asset of our marriage—his newly earned postprofessional degree. I'd put him through school, yet he would keep an earning power that had doubled while my own stood still.

I realize I was one of the very lucky ones. I was young, healthy, and educated. I was also—and this is crucial—childless. I was even a lawyer by profession, so I knew my chances of winning a fairer settlement in court were slim. For a man to leave a marriage far wealthier than his wife is, quite simply, the norm.

In the months that followed, though, a thought haunted me: Suppose I hadn't been white, educated, and financially advantaged? Suppose, more simply, I'd had a child? How much more dangerous the inequities would have been. [Takas, 1986]

ANY DISCUSSION OF DIVORCE, whether serious or casual, inevitably contains some allusion to the financial implications of a divorce decision. In this country, husbands and wives are considered economic units, and when they divorce, economic arrangements must be made (Bohannan, 1970). This involves many areas, including property, children, spousal support, and earning power. For this reason it is often an emotional process and it is not uncommon for couples to experience conflict regarding the economic aspects of divorce. This process has been referred to as a "bloody battle" (Weiss, 1975), and

can be at least partially attributed to the fact that . . . it is possible for one
party to harass the other by means of extortion, threats, punishments,
and attribution. Only the young and childless, those with either little
property and no child custody or support or alimony to fight over . . .
escape conflict. [Hunt and Hunt, 1977: 198]

Economic decisions shape the futures of divorcing spouses and their
children. In spite of the importance of these decisions, economic issues
have historically been ignored or received very little attention. Even
lawyers and counselors have emphasized other areas—often to the
exclusion of the economic issues.

In my experience, most family counselors, psychologists, social workers,
psychiatrists, pastoral counselors, and other members of the "helping
professions" are neither money or business oriented. The counseling
procedure continues to the conclusion without a realistic view of finances
either during the marriage or in the event of divorce. Even lawyers . . .
rarely . . . look past the divorce to a frank discussion of what happens the
morning and years after. [Bernstein, 1977: 421]

Part of this neglect can be the result of the state of "flux" that divorce
laws have been in during the past few decades. For example, guidelines
for monetary decisions related to divorce emerged from English
ecclesiastical law (Brown, 1976) and settlements were often based on
the fault of a spouse (see Chapter 6). With the advent of no-fault divorce
in 1970, combined with changing attitudes about the appropriate roles
of men and women, this pattern has dramatically changed. These
changes are evident in recent research in this area, including Lenore
Weitzman's landmark study that was published in 1985.

MARITAL PROPERTY

Marital property has been traditionally defined as wages and salary
income, interest, dividends, returns on investments, and all other
income either spouse earned during the marriage, as well as any
property that has been purchased with that income (Weitzman, 1985).
The majority of states in this country have a *separate property system,*
that is, assets of each spouse is considered his or her property. The
underlying assumption in this system is that the property belongs to the
spouse who earned it (most often the husband) and the court will decide
what is an equitable share of the property for the other spouse (usually
the wife, who typically receives about one-third of the total property). In
stark contrast, in community property states, the basic premise is

property acquired during marriage (excluding inheritance and gifts) was "earned" by both spouses, regardless of who received the pay-check. Therefore, property is divided equitably—one-half to the wife and one-half to the husband (Weitzman, 1985). These clear differences, however, have been blurred by states adopting equal rights amendments (which give wives access to their husbands' property that was acquired during marriage). Other states have adopted equitable distribution rules for dividing property (Weitzman, 1985).

Most divorcing couples have relatively few monetary assets at the time of divorce and these assets are usually of relatively low value. In addition, very few divorcing men and women have any assets that were acquired before marriage—by gift or inheritance (Goode, 1956; U.S. Bureau of the Census, 1983b; Weitzman, 1985). Most divorcing couples have household furnishings and some form of money (bank accounts, stocks, or bonds). Less than half, however, will own equity in a home, have money in a pension, a business, or additional real estate. Not surprisingly, younger couples have even fewer assets (Weitzman, 1985).

The Division of Marital Property

Under English common law, divorce was not permissible. The ecclesiastical courts could, however, grant separation to an innocent spouse (usually the woman) if there was proof of misconduct. In this case, the husband had to continue to support his wife, because upon marriage her property had become his and she was considered his responsibility.

In the American states, divorce became permissible, but most women, because of their dependent role, continued to require support from their former husbands. Recently, however, because of changes in the roles of women combined with the implementation of no-fault divorce, continued support for the wife has been questioned. For example, in theory, no-fault divorce provides a means for dissolving a partnership of equals (Kurtz, 1977) and, accordingly, marital property should be divided equally (unless a couple agrees to an unequal division). The equal division requirement was instituted in order to (1) rid the legal system of "economic blackmail," (2) protect wives, and (3) limit judicial discretion (Weitzman, 1985).

Judicial discretion is, however, still practiced in those states that have established guidelines for the division of marital property. Such guidelines usually include the financial resources of each spouse, health of each spouse, length of marriage, ability of supported spouse to engage in gainful employment, time needed in order for the spouse seeking maintenance to acquire sufficient education or training to enable him or her to secure employment, wife's work in the home during the marriage, and misconduct (Combs, 1979). However, even in these systems, property is not being divided equally because women are often advised to "trade off" support awards for property. The reason for this exchange is that division of property is a one-time event and a "sure thing," while continued support awards may not be paid (Johnson, 1976; Weitzman, 1985).

The family home. The family's major economic asset is usually the home, and there is a trend toward equal division of the equity in this home. This means a couple can maintain joint ownership after divorce or that the house must be sold and the equity divided equally at the time of divorce. Many women who keep the family home (where she and the couple's children will live) actually pay their husband for his share—possibly with cash or by relinquishing her claim to a comparable asset, such as the husband's retirement pension (Seal, 1979). However, in most families there are no other assets to trade (Weitzman, 1985); therefore, a home would have to be sold, even if there were minor children. In these cases, the custodial parent (usually the mother) is confronted with finding adequate housing for her family, often at a higher cost than expenses on the family home.

Division of other assets. Sex typing of awards still exists; women continue more often to be awarded the family home and furnishings, whereas husbands are more likely to be awarded the business and the family car (if the family has only one car). In dividing a couple's assets after a divorce, there is still an assumption that the business belongs to the husband, and the courts automatically assume the business is equal in value to the price of the family home (Weitzman, 1985).

Men, because of their work patterns, are more likely than women to have pensions. If both spouses have pensions, they are likely to be awarded their own pensions. However, in other cases, pensions are awarded to the worker, with comparable monetary awards to the other spouse. If money, stocks, and bonds are available, they are often used to offset other awards and equalize the division of property (Weitzman, 1985). However, in many families these other assets are not available and, in either case, women are often forced to relinquish the future security of a retirement income in the process of dividing assets.

Men are more often ordered to pay the couple's debts, even though this practice is decreasing. However, if this is the case, the husband is generally compensated for this expenditure by being awarded other property of equal value (Weitzman, 1985).

The Internal Revenue Service (IRS) is also interested in how a divorcing couple's property is divided. The tax considerations are crucial if large amounts of property exist. Accountants often have an active role in working with divorce attorneys and couples to arrive at the best tax arrangement. A key issue in this area is how to transfer property in a way to avoid paying capital gains taxes. In general, the IRS treats property transferred in a divorce as if it is sold, even though no money has changed hands; that is, appreciating assets (house, stocks) are subject to capital gains taxes (Feld, 1976; Harmelink and Shurtz, 1977; Lavoie, 1978).

The New Property

The "new property" is defined as pensions, education, and other career assets (Weitzman, 1985). Increasingly, social scientists, consumer economists, legislatures, and judicial systems view several components of the "new property" as part of the pool of marital assets to be divided upon divorce (Combs, 1979; Smith and Beninger, 1982; Weitzman, 1985). The rationale behind this position is that couples actually acquire career assets much the same way they acquire tangible assets.

Equality in the division of family assets upon divorce has been implemented in some areas, but not in others; that is, marital assets and debts are being equally divided when equality is still lacking in employment opportunities, child rearing, and job preparation (Seal, 1979). In both single-career and two-career families, the husband's career more often has priority. Couples devote time, money, and energy to building this career, and it is not unusual for the wife to postpone or abandon her own education or career aspirations in order to put her husband through school or to help advance his career (Smith and Beninger, 1982; Weitzman, 1985). Consequently, it is the husband who possesses the family's assets, which not only include education, training, licensing, and so forth, but also the experience, the network of contacts, insurance (health, hospital, and life), unemployment and social security benefits, as well as pensions or retirement benefits. Because of both spouse's contributions, these assets are viewed as an investment they both made and, therefore, an asset to be divided (Combs, 1979; Weitzman, 1985).

TRANSFER OF MONEY

Alimony

In the past (if not present) women were encouraged to devote themselves to their husbands, children, and homes. In return, their husbands were expected to support them. If they divorced, alimony was expected to be paid. This system:

(1) reinforced the husband's continuing obligation to provide for his wife
(2) rewarded virtue and punished wrongdoing
(3) reinforced the belief women were entitled to live the same lifestyle after divorce they lived while married
(4) compensated the wife for her labor during marriage
(5) reinforced the concept of sharing, pooling, and partnership in marriage (Weitzman, 1985)

Alimony has been referred to as a *maintenance allowance, support, separate maintenance, rehabilitative alimony,* and *spousal support.* Unlike the former attitude that husbands should continue to support their wives after divorce, today there are three basic criteria used in determining alimony awards (McCubbin and Dahl, 1985):

(1) The moral conduct of the husband and wife that comes to the court's attention even in the present "no-fault" era. Thus an innocent wife may receive more than a wife whose character is in question.
(2) Needs of the wife. The level of education, vocational training, health, age, and number of children are major considerations in the amount and duration of spousal support.
(3) Ability of the husband to pay. Courts are reluctant to assess a man more than he can realistically pay because of the high rate of default and difficulty of enforcement.

Under this system, while a woman has to show she is unable to support herself, there are three groups who are viewed as having compelling financial needs (Weitzman, 1985):

(1) those with custodial responsibility for children
(2) those who require transitional support to become self-supporting
(3) those who are incapable of becoming or are too old to become self-supporting (p. 149)

Based on these premises, one might assume women, and particularly women with younger children and older women, automatically receive alimony. Facts, however, do not substantiate this assumption. For example, Weitzman (1981, 1985) reported that during the period from 1887 to 1906, only 9.3% of all divorced women were awarded alimony; in 1922, 14.7%; and in 1977, 16%. While there were 17 million divorced or separated women in the United States in the spring of 1982, only 15% had been awarded alimony payments (U.S. Bureau of the Census, 1983b). Therefore, under the no-fault system of divorce, not only does a lower percentage of women receive alimony, there has been a shift from "permanent" to short-term "transitional" awards. For example, in the state of California during 1977, the duration of transitional alimony awards was 25 months—the implication being that a woman can and should be self-sufficient in that period of time (Weitzman, 1985). In addition, the amount of alimony awarded is often too meager to be considered a legitimate means of support. The mean amount of alimony received by women in 1981 was approximately $3,000 per year (U.S. Bureau of the Census, 1983b). Furthermore, few husbands pay the decreed award on a regular basis, that is, 43% of all women due alimony payments in 1981 received full payment (U.S. Bureau of the Census, 1983b). Consequently, women are thrown into the labor market without sufficient job skills or time to develop skills needed to improve their long-term economic prospects. In addition, alimony has practically been eliminated for women married less than five years.

Starting in 1977, husbands became eligible for alimony or spousal support based on the same criteria applied to wives. The Supreme Court viewed the traditional notion that the husband is primarily responsible for providing for the household as discriminatory (Oakland, 1984). For example, a small but increasing number of men abandon careers for full-time homemaking and child rearing.

Child Support

In 1982, 80% of all divorced mothers with custody of their children had been awarded child support (U.S. Bureau of the Census, 1983a, 1983b). The average amount of these awards was approximately $4,000 per year and averaged about 13% of the father's income (in both 1978 and 1981), with men earning lower incomes paying a greater proportion of their incomes in child support (Weitzman, 1985). Regardless of income, however, divorced men are rarely ordered to pay more than one-third of their net income in support of their divorced family. This is attributed to the "father first" principle; that is, children get what is left after money is set aside for his needs (Eisler, 1977). The importance of this principle may be to protect the father's ability to pay by not making the award too burdensome, thus leaving him with enough money to motivate him to earn (Weitzman, 1985).

Three criteria can be used to determine the adequacy of child support awards: (1) the actual costs of raising children, (2) the reasonableness of the awards in terms of the father's financial resources, and (3) the financial contribution of the two parents in terms of the money they contribute (Weitzman, 1985).

Several methods have been used to estimate the cost of raising a child. The USDA (Edwards, 1985) conservatively estimated the cost for a moderate-income family to raise a child to be approximately $96,000. In contrast, *Parents Magazine* considered the age of the child and the impact of inflation, and calculated that it costs over $175,000 (Tilling, 1980). Assuming a second child increases these costs by about 50%, and using the USDA's conservative figure, it can cost approximately $7,000 to $9,000 per year to raise two children. Therefore, it is safe to say child support awards are generally not adequate to cover the costs of raising a child.

If a family's income remains constant after divorce, both spouses cannot maintain their previous standard of living. However, paying child support may not economically deprive fathers. Even if men complied with child support awards, most can still live at or above the government's intermediate standard budget level (Espenshade, 1979). In contrast, it is the wife and children who experience a lowered standard of living. For example, in Michigan, even if fathers paid the full amount of ordered child support, 97% of the divorced women and children would be living below the poverty line (Chambers, 1979); in California, only 7% of the women and children would be living at the same level as before the divorce, whereas 93% would be living below the poverty level (Weitzman, 1985).

When considering the contributions of both parents toward raising the child, the custodial parent's (usually the mother's) contribution in terms of time and child care services are usually not considered. These services are not monetary contributions. If these contributions were included, fathers would definitely not be contributing an equal share. Therefore, the custodial parent, who generally has less earning capacity and less ability to pay, ends up paying a disproportionately larger share of the cost of child support.

In increasing numbers of cases where fathers are granted custody of their children, the wife/mother is required to pay child support, especially if she has an adequate income. The child support obligation on the part of either father or mother is expected to be maintained regardless of whether the custodial parent remarries.

The Erosion of Child Support

Several factors, including inflation and a child's growing up, may change or restructure the original support order (Eden, 1979). The result is the custodial parent has to repeatedly return to court in order to have the original child support order modified (Seal, 1979), or survive on less and less money. Few attorneys want to take these cases unless the custodial parent has other resources or the amount of child support is extremely high (Eisler, 1977). In addition, some private attorneys want "up front" money—often in the amount the noncustodial parent is behind in support payments.

An alternative to the continuing erosion of child support awards is for the original order to take into account circumstances beyond the time of the decision. This is not a new idea. Divorcing people have been cautioned to have automatic clauses specified in the initial settlement and stipulations that spell out future conditions (Blackwell, 1977). Two of these conditions are inflation and the growth of a child:

> It is hard to see how a child support order can fail to make allowance for the growth of a child and the increased costs associated with that growth. There is nothing speculative or uncertain about this . . . child support schedules with automatic increases should be devised to allow for this fact of life. With but rare exceptions, since the beginning of this century, we have had continuous inflation . . . it is time we accepted this basic characteristic of our economic system and recognized it in writing support orders. [Eden, 1979: 4-5]

In order to determine the amount of the original child support award and to justify why monetary increases should be included in this agreement, several factors need to be considered (Price-Bonham and Bonham, 1982). These include: (1) Living expenses for the child or children should be itemized. These figures can be secured from checkbooks, income tax records, and expense ledgers. For the purposes of expediency, these should be tabulated on a monthly basis and subsequently annualized (see Table 7.1).

Possible changes in living expenses that may occur as the result of the divorce should be determined. Expenditures for such items as transportation, entertainment, vacations, and clothing may be reduced because the noncustodial parent is out of the household. However, expenses including housing, utilities, medical care, education, automobile, taxes, and most types of insurance will probably remain unchanged, whereas other expenses, including child care, can definitely increase.

(2) The impact inflation will have on the amount of the original child support award should be determined because inflation ravages the purchasing power of any award. A custodial mother who was awarded child support in the amount of $500 per month in 1977 experienced a continuous decline in purchasing power each of the next nine years. For 1985-1986, this $500 award amounted to $298.47! The total loss in purchasing power for those nine years was over $13,000, or over 24% of the total child support payment, as presented in Table 7.2.

(3) The impact of the age of the child or children on costs of raising a child needs to be determined. As children grow, their needs increase,

TABLE 7.1
Items That May Be Included in Child's Living Expenses

A. Housing	D. Clothing	G. Miscellaneous
rent	clothes	babysitter
house payment	shoes	child care
repair and upkeep	accessories	school
housekeeper	laundry	school supplies
yard work	cleaning	newspapers
insurance	other	magazines
taxes		books
other	E. Medical	dues
	physician	allowances
B. Utilities	dentist	recreation
sewer	drugs	entertainment
electricity	medical supplies	pets
gas	insurance	gifts
telephone	optical	life insurance
garbage	other	lessons
other		other
	F. Transportation	
C. Food	car payment	
groceries	maintenance	
milk	insurance	
household supplies	gas/oil	
school lunches	bus fare	
meals outside home	parking	
other	other	

SOURCE: Adapted from Price-Bonham and Bonham (1982) and Sylvan (1982).

including their tendency to eat more and wear more expensive clothing. For example, the cost of raising a 17-year-old child is about 50% more than for a 1-year-old child (Eden, 1979). Based on estimates from the U.S. Department of Agriculture, in 1985 the estimated average cost of rearing one child on a moderate budget in an urban area ranged from $4,597 per year for a 1-year-old to $6,410 for a 17-year-old (Edwards, 1985) (see Table 7.3). The combined impact of the growth of a child and inflation will magnify these expenses.

Compliance with Child Support Awards

The widespread lack of compliance with court-ordered child support awards has been well documented and publicized (Weitzman, 1981, 1985). A 1978 survey conducted by the U.S. Bureau of the Census revealed one-half of the women who were awarded child support received it as ordered, one-quarter of the women received less than the full amount, and one-quarter never received a single payment (U.S. Bureau of the Census, 1983b). Similarly, in California, within one year after divorce, one-third of the custodial mothers reported they regularly received the full amount of court-ordered child support, 43% reported receiving little or no child support, and 22% reported having problems in either obtaining the full amount of the order or obtaining it on time (Weitzman, 1981, 1985).

TABLE 7.2
Difference in Purchasing Power of $500/Month at 5.9% Inflation Rate

End of Year	Average Monthly Purchasing Power ($)	Average Less per Month ($)	Annual Loss ($)
1	472.14	27.86	334.32
2	445.84	54.16	649.92
3	421.00	79.00	948.00
4	397.55	102.45	1,229.40
5	375.40	124.60	1,495.20
6	354.48	145.52	1,746.24
7	334.73	165.27	1,983.24
8	316.08	183.92	2,207.04
9	298.47	201.53	2,418.38
Total loss			13,011.74

NOTE: Based on 5.9% average inflation rate 1977-78 through 1985-86, calculated by authors.

Three additional studies that investigated compliance with child support awards are the 1975 Survey of Income and Education (SIE), the March 1979 supplement to the Current Population Survey (CPS), and the 1977 AFDC survey (Sorenson and McDonald, 1982). The SIE, conducted in 1976, provides data on child support payments during 1975 for about 5,000 women; the CPS, conducted in 1979, provides data on child support payments for 7,000 women during 1978; and the AFDC survey consists of a sample of case histories reported by AFDC caseworkers.

These studies indicated that only a minority of demographically eligible women received child support payments: 25% of the women in the SIE study, 35% of the women in the CPS study, and 10.5% of the AFDC women. In addition, Black women were less than half as likely to receive child support as White women, and women with the fewest years of schooling were the least likely to receive child support.

The research on compliance with child support awards points to three consistent findings:

(1) Not one study has found a state or county in which more than one-half of the fathers fully complied with court orders.

TABLE 7.3
Cost of Rearing an Urban Child per Year
by Age of Child in 1985, Moderate-Cost Level

Age of Child	Mean Annual Cost ($)
less than 1	4,597
1	4,740
2	4,489
3	4,489
4	4,739
5	4,739
6	5,043
7	5,218
8	5,218
9	5,218
10	5,432
11	5,432
12	5,768
13	5,910
14	5,910
15	5,910
16	6,410
17	6,410
Total	$95,672

SOURCE: Adapted from Edwards (1985).
NOTE: Includes home-produced food and food away from home, clothing, housing, medical care, education, transportation, and miscellaneous expenses.

(2) Many of the fathers who are ordered to pay support pay it irregularly and are often in arrears.
(3) A very sizable minority of fathers—between a quarter and a third—never make a single court-ordered payment (Weitzman, 1985).

Some of the literature appears to point to the conclusion that fathers cannot afford to pay child support as ordered by the court (Weiss, 1984). However, the Michigan Study (Chambers, 1979) and Weitzman (1981, 1985) found divorced fathers, in general, are able to live quite well after making these payments. Weitzman (1985) also reported that only

8% of the fathers in her study with incomes of $50,000 or above were irregular with their payments or made no payments. In contrast, she reported 27% of the men who made less than $10,000 per year fell into this category; 27% of the men who made $10,000-20,000; 22% of those who made $20,000-30,000; and 29% of those fathers who made $30,000-50,000 per year. Failure to pay is often attributed to (a) the noncustodial father's feeling of emotional distance from his children and/or (b) remarriage making it economically and psychological burdensome to support two households (Wallerstein and Kelly, 1980). In contrast, Wright and Price (1986) reported the relationship between former spouses was a major factor in whether noncustodial fathers complied with court-ordered child support awards. Specifically, those non-custodial fathers who remained attached to their former spouses more often pay child support as decreed.

Enforcement of Compliance

There has been a dramatic increase in the range of actions available to ensure compliance with child support awards (both within and across state lines) during the past few years. However, judges and attorneys may be reluctant to use them (Weitzman, 1985).

A self-starting system and a high incarceration rate appear to be related to the highest levels of compliance (Chambers, 1979). In the self-starting system, child support payments are made directly to the court, and as soon as a father is delinquent, action is implemented by the court and does not wait for a complaint from the mother. In addition, if there is a high probability of jail for continuously delinquent fathers, the compliance rates are higher. It should be noted, however, that some men pay as well as they are able without any threats, whereas others are so unable to pay that the threat of jail does not produce additional benefits (Chambers, 1979).

In 1982, federal legislation was strengthened by establishing a Parent Locater Service, available to custodial parents of children on welfare, with access to various government record-keeping systems, including the IRS. Consequently, fathers who had moved to another state can be located, and federal income-tax refunds can be intercepted to cover past-due support (Weitzman, 1985).

In 1984, the Child Support Enforcement Amendment was passed. This strengthened the 1982 law in several respects:

(1) Middle-class families are allowed access to the IRS's locater and tax refund intercept services and states are encouraged to collect past-due child support for families who are not on welfare, thereby admitting noncompliance is not just a welfare problem.

(2) A mandate for wage attachment is provided.
(3) States are required to establish procedures for expediting the imposition of liens against property and the posting of bonds to guarantee payment of overdue support.
(4) States are required to intercept state tax refunds (in addition to the federal tax intercept program).
(5) States are required to provide information on past-due child support to consumer credit agencies when the past-due amount is over $1,000.
(6) States are required to seek medical support as part of child support whenever health insurance for dependent children is available to the noncustodial parent.
(7) An option is provided for having payments made through a state agency—at the request of either parent.
(8) States are required to publicize the availability of child support enforcement services.
(9) States are required to establish specific guidelines for child support awards through legislative, judicial, and administrative action. Such guidelines, however, are not binding on judges and will therefore not guarantee uniform award levels (Weitzman, 1985).

ECONOMIC CONSEQUENCES OF DIVORCE

There are several unintended consequences that have resulted from the impact of divorce on economic well-being. It has been repeatedly documented that men fare better economically after divorce than women and that women fare particularly poorly under no-fault divorce (Dixon and Weitzman, 1980; Seal, 1979; Weitzman, 1981, 1985; Welch and Price-Bonham, 1983). In California, after calculating a family's predivorce budget level, the wife's postdivorce family budget level, and the husband's postdivorce family budget level, and comparing these three budgets to the needs of each family, men experienced a 42% improvement in their postdivorce standard of living, whereas women experienced a 73% decline (Weitzman, 1985).

This reduction in economic resources for women has resulted in the "feminization of poverty," or the new poor. Indicative of the lowered standard of living for women are displaced homemakers, increased levels of employment by women, and increased demands on welfare.

Displaced Homemakers

A displaced homemaker is an individual who has, for a substantial number of years, provided unpaid service to her family and has been dependent on her spouse for her income, but who, in this case, has lost her spouse through divorce (Shields, 1981). Most of these women are over 40 and have adhered to the belief that their husbands would be the breadwinner and they the homemaker. However, the rise in no-fault divorce, the decrease in community disapproval of divorce, and the possibility of dissolution on demand by one spouse have resulted in 20% of today's divorces involving marriages of more than 15 years duration (Weitzman, 1985). As a result of the vast changes in our society and in the roles and expectations of women, less than one-half of these women receive any support after divorce. Most live on a small percentage of their previous family income, and many have no security of an income when they reach retirement age (Corcoran, 1979). Very few of these women have held full-time, long-term jobs, and many have not worked since the early years of their marriage, if at all. Consequently, they do not have marketable job skills or their job skills are long outdated, and they are unable to find a job other than for minimum wages.

> Employers do not recognize homemaking skills as having a market value. They only recognize "recent paid work experience" and even with such experience, older women are unwanted in today's labor market. [Weitzman, 1985: 209]

Employment

Typically, child support awards are insufficient to cover even half of the costs of raising a child. Consequently, by necessity the majority of divorced women must seek employment not only to support themselves but also to support their children. Judges may actually believe a divorced woman should work instead of staying home with her children because (a) it is good for a divorced woman to earn money instead of continuing dependency on her former husband, (b) work is seen as a form of rehabilitation that will help the divorced woman build a new life, (c) the combination of work and motherhood is viewed as normal for a divorced woman, and (d) her former husband cannot earn enough to support her (Weitzman, 1985).

As a result, many divorced women must pursue whatever job they can get or even work at two jobs in order to support their family. This practice is often not the best solution because women who obtain job counseling, enroll in training programs, and delay entry into the labor force for a year or more after divorce are more successful in both job levels and earnings (Mott and Moore, 1979).

Because of the pressures imposed by single parenting combined with holding down a job, many single mothers suffer from "role overload." These women report they feel "frightened," "that life is hard," "rushed," "worried about a nervous breakdown," and "worried about bills" more than any other group of American men and women (Campbell et al.,

1976). Divorced mothers report carrying out hectic and exhausting schedules. The pressure to earn money leaves them little time for child care, household chores, or a social life. Children are dropped off at the baby-sitters early in the morning and picked up on the way home at night. Some mothers have to work past midnight on a regular basis in order to complete their household chores. As a result of this overload, the children not only have less of their fathers, but also less of their mothers (Wallerstein and Kelly, 1980). This stressful lifestyle does not apply only to lower-income women. For example, Wallerstein and Kelly (1980) reported the following:

> The decline in the standard of living was made more troublesome for some women by the way it brought them into a lower socioeconomic class. Women who had been in the highest and most prosperous socioeconomic group, in particular, faced an entirely changed life. For these women, all of them left by their husbands, the moorings of their identification with a certain social class, and with it the core of their self-esteem—formerly exclusively determined by the husband's education, occupation, and income—were shaken loose. [1980: 231]

Therefore, it is not surprising, divorced women report high levels of stress. This stress is increased by the lack of social networks as they are often excluded from their former networks and have fewer resources and time to develop new ones (Arendell, 1986; Brandwein et al., 1974).

Welfare

Female-headed families constituted 15% of all American households in 1980, but 50% of those with incomes below the poverty level (U.S. Bureau of Census, 1983a). It is not uncommon for divorced mothers to receive welfare and food stamps after divorce. These sources of income are used by women in all social classes, but particularly by mothers whose predivorce family income was in the lower-income brackets. This outside income provides as much as 75% of the postdivorce family's income (Weiss, 1984). (Older women with no dependent children would not be eligible for welfare programs.)

Whether or not a woman receives child support determines, to a significant degree, whether or not she applies for public assistance. In a 1978 census sample, 38% of women without child support from the father of their children received public assistance, compared to only 13% of the women receiving child support income (U.S. Bureau of the Census, 1979). The fact that women are severely limited in what they can earn without losing part or all of their welfare assistance makes this situation even worse.

•

SUMMARY

Economics is a major concern in the divorce process because it has an adverse impact on many families, particularly divorced mothers and their children. It is critical that changing divorce laws and the changing roles of women be considered when attempting to determine the economic impact of divorce. In reality, we are punishing older women for doing what society told them was appropriate, and, likewise, are punishing younger women for having children.

In view of the economic impact of divorce on women, it is necessary today for women to prepare to be self-sufficient and able to support not only themselves but their children as well. No-fault divorce laws appear to be more appropriate and fair to a new generation of working women. These women may experience discomfort as a result of the transition to a single-income household, but they should not be on the brink of financial disaster as a result of divorce, as older displaced homemakers often are.

REVIEW QUESTIONS

1. How do separate property states and community property states differ in the division of marital property upon divorce?
2. What has been the impact of no-fault divorce on the economic well-being of women and children?
3. What are the methods used to determine the amount of child support awards? What factors should be considered in determining a child support award?
4. What property is generally divided at the time of divorce and, in general, how is it divided? What is meant by the "new property?"
5. How has recent legislation strengthened efforts to ensure compliance with child support awards?

SUGGESTED PROJECTS

1. Write an article in which you advise young women how to prepare themselves for the possibility of being a divorced parent.
2. Contact various community agencies in your community. Find out what programs are available for displaced homemakers or for women who are divorced but have no job skills.
3. Develop a budget for a custodial parent and two small children. Using this budget, determine how much child support the noncustodial parent should pay.

CHAPTER

8

Intervention and Divorce

Society provides widow's weeds and black arm bands for those who have lost a spouse through death, but has nothing to say to the increasing numbers of men and women who need help in getting through the emotional crisis of divorce. [Krantzler, 1973: 31]

THE SIGNIFICANT INCREASE in the number of individuals affected by divorce in recent years has not been accompanied by widespread societal support that might ease the transition from a married to a single or a remarried lifestyle. This lack of support has been attributed, in part, to the stigma attached to "divorced" status. In fact, punishment or isolation, not help, has been a more typical societal response to divorcing individuals. In addition, helping professionals have been traditionally trained and philosophically oriented toward strategies to strengthen marriage and thereby prevent divorce, and not toward approaches to facilitate postdivorce adjustment. Many helping professionals have had to reconcile their personal and professional attitudes toward divorce because of the vast numbers of individuals in need of help in coping with the many transitions associated with divorce. Some sources have emerged in recent years to help individuals and families cope with divorce-related issues, including individual, marriage, family, or group counseling and therapy, as well as informal peer support groups, clergy, divorce mediation, and educational programs. The primary goal of these approaches is to assist individuals through the separation process and to facilitate the establishment of a stable identity.

WHO SEEKS HELP

It is difficult to estimate the number of individuals seeking professional assistance with divorce-related emotional problems. However, Kressel et al. (1978) estimate that approximately 15% of all divorced individuals receive some form of counseling during the divorce process, and this trend appears to be increasing. Kressel et al. also note that the majority of professional contacts are really pro forma—the result of either the need to assuage a guilty conscience or a court regulation requiring conciliation counseling. This figure, however, excludes informal social supports, including friends and relatives, which are far more commonly used than professionals. For example, Chiriboga et al. (1979) found that less than 20% of divorcing individuals sought no help, and that the majority turned to more than one category of helper; the most frequent sources of help were friends, spouses, counselors (an inclusive term), and relatives—in that order.

Women are far more likely than men to seek professional assistance, partially resulting from being socialized to acknowledge emotional distress and to seek help and support from others. Men's greater distress during separation may, in fact, be linked to the socialization of males to be emotionally inexpressive and to solve their personal problems independently.

Other family members, especially children, are also likely to need professional assistance; however, existing services for children are grossly inadequate. Also, intervention approaches for extended family members are minimal. This reflects society's inability to recognize that extended family members, including parents of the divorced, can also be very affected by divorce.

DIVORCE COUNSELING

Divorce counseling can be defined as a therapeutic process that (a) aids those people considering divorce and/or those divorcing in determining whether their needs can be met within marriage, and (b) assists them in the process of divorce (Brown, 1976). However, because divorce counseling is in a transitional stage of development, its practice varies among practitioners (Kressel & Deutsch, 1977). For example, divorce counseling may be offered by counselors or therapists in private practice, social service agencies, conciliation counselors, marriage and family therapists, clergy, or divorce mediators. (It should be noted that while many professionals make a distinction between counseling and therapy, the literature tends to use the term "divorce counseling" to refer to both.) Regardless of professional orientation, it is necessary for persons offering divorce counseling to accept divorce as a rational alternative. Divorce counseling also carries with it some other basic assumptions that may conflict with the views of marriage and family held by practitioners. Divorce counselors are compelled to accept the fact that divorce does not necessarily dissolve the family unit and that a variety of individual and family lifestyles may constitute functional living arrangements (Brown, 1976).

Divorce counseling is often considered a form of marriage and family counseling, yet it differs from marriage and family counseling in four respects:

(1) divorce counseling may focus more on the individual then a family
(2) divorce counseling aims to decrease the functions of a relationship with the goal of eventual dissolution
(3) divorce counseling promotes personal growth, not adjustment
(4) divorce counseling assumes that divorcing people are normal people in crisis, not individuals suffering from psychopathology (Brown, 1976)

Many divorce counselors practice under the title of "marriage counselor." From a consumer perspective, Fisher (1974) suggests, however, that that title is misleading, as it portrays an image of marriage preservation. Instead, she advocates the title "marriage and divorce counseling," as it conveys a more open and helping attitude, regardless of the ultimate decision.

The emergence of divorce counseling as a specialty has been accompanied by a proliferation of related literature. However, systematic research in this area is lacking. Kressel and Deutsch (1977) contend that the role of the therapist in divorce is the most underrepresented area of clinical research. Consequently, while it is clear that divorce counseling is an increasingly popular alternative, exact frequencies of use, techniques, and evaluations are only beginning to appear in the literature.

Different theoretical approaches and strategies, however, have been published. Many of these are developmental in nature, utilizing established techniques to help individuals and/or couples "work through" the loss or losses that divorce represents (Salts, 1979), while others focus on ways to facilitate a client's gradual acceptance of loss after having experienced the emotional stages of divorce, such as denial, anger, and depression (e.g., Rice, 1979). Several writers have outlined specific goals and strategies according to the stage of the divorce process, rather than the emotional stage of the individual. For example, Brown (1976) emphasizes the need for divorce counseling during the decision-making and restructuring periods; Fisher (1974) delineates three distinct periods (predivorce, during litigation, and after divorce); and Levy and Joffe (1978) emphasize the periods of separation, individuation, and reconnection. As both Fisher, and Levy and Joffe note, each phase of divorce involves a unique matrix of needs, anxieties, and potentials for personal growth (see Figure 4.1) .

Divorce counselors have to be cognizant of the many practical areas facing their divorcing clients, such as economics, family law, and parent-child relationships. In particular, Kressel (1980) stresses that the divorce counselor can be most effective by combining concrete and practical forms of assistance with their therapeutic role in the divorce decision-making process. He suggests that counselors become informed in legal and economic issues in order to play an active role in both the decision to divorce as well as the litigation process. Specifically, women often need help in dealing with such practical issues as finances and vocational planning.

Granvold (1983) takes a more behavioral approach to divorce counseling through the use of a "separation contract." The behavioral contract has become a popular contemporary tool for clarifying interactions over a broad range of situations; it is specifically used in divorce counseling to provoke thought and action toward divorce or reconciliation. The use of a behavioral contract requires couples who are in the process of deciding about divorce to commit to a moratorium on a final decision. With guidance, the couple writes the separation contract, specifying expected behaviors in such areas as duration of separation, frequency of contact, sexual contact with spouse and others, and contact with children. Couples are expected to participate in weekly conjoint therapy, with accompanying individual therapy and homework assignments. In addition, the noncustodial parent is expected to continue regular contact with the children and maintain customary financial obligations.

GROUP APPROACHES

Consistent with the trend toward less expensive, short-term, and problem-specific treatments, group intervention approaches have become very popular with divorcing/divorced persons (Granvold and Welch, 1977). Group approaches include therapy groups where principles of divorce counseling are practiced, self-help support groups, and groups that are more didactic and educational in nature.

Educational groups became popular in the 1960s as the number of divorced individuals dramatically increased. These groups typically focus on helping divorced individuals gain mastery over their environment and gain more self-confidence. They usually assume the format of short lectures, followed by group discussion, and are often leaderless or led by a layperson. These groups are often sponsored by churches, women's groups, various community organizations, or organizations with a specific interest in divorce, such as Parents Without Partners.

Educational groups may also take the form of workshops, which focus on topics such as legal services, child custody, vocational planning, and managing finances. They may also follow a lecture-discussion model that emphasizes the psychology of adjustment in the grief-loss process and provides practical information. Regardless of focus, these groups generally stop short of formal counseling or therapy, but readily refer members to appropriate professionals as needed.

Self-help groups constitute another approach to helping divorcing individuals. While these groups may have an educational focus, they exist primarily to offer emotional support to their members. Although there are many variations, these groups are primarily directed toward the recently separated or divorced, who need encouragement, hope, and enhancement of their self-esteem. Members take full responsibility for any program and overall leadership in these groups. For example, "We Care" self-help groups began in Minneapolis in the 1960s and rapidly spread to other cities nationwide.

Consciousness-raising groups are one popular variation of the self-help group. These are usually small groups of 6 to 10 members, usually women, who meet without a leader to discuss whatever issues or problems are important to its members at the time. Women who have utilized such groups have reported increased self-esteem as well as learning they can draw on group support when isolation, frustration, resentment, and guilt associated with divorce become overwhelming.

Professional counselors have found the group approach especially helpful to divorcing individuals who suffer from social isolation and loneliness. Through this approach, divorced individuals become part of a network of social relationships and experience a sense of belonging to a group of peers. Groups have an advantage over individual approaches because members have the opportunity to learn from the experiences of others and to get immediate feedback from peers.

Proponents of structured group approaches emphasize the efficiency of structured settings with emphasis on working through various issues through such exercises as role playing, writing, giving feedback, and nonverbal exercises (Kessler, 1978). In contrast, proponents of unstructured groups argue that ambiguity of such groups allows members to work through their period of dependency on their leader, their subsequent rebellion, and their final conflict resolution. Kessler, in one of the few systematic evaluations of the group approach, found that structured groups, compared to unstructured groups, were more effective in helping persons regain their self-confidence and emotional autonomy, as well as in gaining a better sense of self-mastery. She concluded that the ambiguity of an unstructured group may only add to the total sense of ambiguity the divorced person often feels. Similarly, Salts and Zongker (1983), in a review of evaluation studies of group approaches, concluded that while group counseling facilitates post-divorce adjustment, structured groups tend to be more effective than unstructured ones.

THE CLERGY

When individuals seek help with a marital problem, they are about twice as likely to consult a member of the clergy as any other helping professional. Until fairly recently, divorce was viewed in most churches as a serious moral failure and betrayal of one's faith. Consequently, faced with vast numbers of their congregation seeking help, clergy have been struggling to find ways to continue to value the permanence of the marriage commitment, while being more sensitive to the need of many divorcing and divorced persons for a new lifestyle and therapeutic assistance with divorce (Young, 1978).

While clergy's activities are much akin to the counselor in that they focus on reducing emotional turmoil, building self-esteem, and pro-moting psychological insight, they do not impartially enter the counseling relationship since they often advocate for one spouse. In addition, reconciliation is often a goal, and religious guidance usually accompanies any counseling.

Clergy may also differ procedurally from counselors in that they (a) may initiate contact, (b) are more prone to use short-term, reality therapy as opposed to insight therapy, and (c) are more informal in their overall approach (Weinglass et al., 1978). Churches also provide much informal support and sometimes professional counseling through their sponsorship of various groups and educational programs that focus on divorce-related issues.

THE LEGAL SYSTEM

The legal system has also responded to the increasing divorce rate with various intervention mechanisms closely akin to the philosophy of divorce counseling. Many judges and attorneys have recognized that counseling assistance in family decision making can reduce conflict surrounding divorce. They have observed that families who leave the court in conflict are likely to return to act out pent-up conflicts and anger (Elkin, 1977). Through such channels as conciliation courts, divorce mediation, and the therapeutic attorney role, the legal system has moved forward in the last decade to deal with some of the emotional needs of divorcing individuals and their families.

Conciliation Courts

As the name implies, conciliation courts have traditionally existed for the purpose of helping separated couples reconcile and preserve their troubled marriages. However, in recent years these courts have recognized the inevitability of divorce and have begun to offer various forms of divorce counseling to facilitate the divorce process. Some courts have established their own counseling offices; others have sponsored counseling services that are independently administered and insulated from the legal process. Some states or jurisdictions now require participation if the divorce involves children, but most offer voluntarily counseling to facilitate the divorce decision or to provide support and guidance during the period of divorce adjustment (Brown and Manela, 1977a).

Most court counselors use a rather structured approach. Typically, the counseling services follow a model of brief-contact, reality-oriented crisis counseling. The approach is thus time-limited, and involves individuals, couples, children, and other family members as warranted. Custody and visitation issues appear to be the most common problems.

The Conciliation Court of Santa Clara, California, instituted in 1972 is representative of those courts that refer child custody and visitation cases to counselors for decision making. Referred couples complete an intake form providing the counselor with needed background information about the family. Attorneys for both sides are then interviewed, issues are presented, and the role of the counselor is explained. The spouses are seen together, often with their children. The goal of this process is to assist the parents in negotiating an agreement they can accept as both functional and consistent with their children's needs and best interests. Most couples are reasonably cooperative as indicated by the fact that fewer than 10% of the cases fail to reach an agreement.

Following the decision-making process, the attorneys, clients, and counselor meet. At this time, the counselor recites his or her understanding of the terms of the agreement. A draft is then prepared, and the parties return to court for approval of the agreement by the judge, which then takes the form of a court order. When the parties cannot agree on a solution, the counselor makes independent recommendations to the court (Weiss and Collada, 1977).

The Wayne County Circuit Court Marriage Counseling Service of Detroit, Michigan, offers voluntary marriage and divorce counseling to individuals and couples on a sliding fee basis. It is more representative of the type of service that might be obtained from a counseling center or through counselors/therapists in private practice. Its goals are to explore options for reconciliation, help individuals understand what went wrong in their marriage, facilitate divorce adjustment, and lessen traumatic effects of divorce on children. The counseling provided is directive, pinpointing problems, making suggestions, giving advice, making referrals, and providing skill training in communication and problem solving. A systematic assessment of this program indicated that approximately 75% of the participants found it helpful (Brown and Manela, 1977a).

Overall, the results of the evaluations of various conciliation court divorce counseling programs have been rather positive. Studies have found that participants in conciliation court counseling are generally very satisfied with the counseling and report more positive attitudes toward their former spouses as a result of the service (Sprenkle and Storm, 1983).

While apparently a successful approach, representatives from both the legal and counseling professions have raised issues about court-related counseling. For example, some legal professionals are resistant to the authority they lose to nonlegal professionals such as counselors. Some counselors are opposed to these programs because of the variability in the qualifications and experience of the counselors. The counseling profession has also traditionally questioned the ethics and the effectiveness of such compulsory counseling programs. Some in the counseling profession contend that such programs violate an individual's privacy and freedom and that two basic characteristics of a successful counseling relationship, motivation and trust, are very difficult to achieve under such conditions (Sonne, 1974).

Divorce Mediation

The formal use of mediators to assist in the resolution of disputes has a long and respected history in such areas as labor-management bargaining, international disputes, and community conflicts. The use of formal mediation in an interpersonal process such as divorce is less common but rapidly growing and gaining respect among legal and mental health professionals. This approach evolved from (a) the divorce counseling programs of conciliation courts, (b) the use of divorce counseling by counselors in private practice, (c) concern that traditional adversarial legal procedures are not the most effective means of resolving divorce disputes, and (d) recognition that the negotiation of details of any divorce settlement, such as alimony, child support, and property division, can be a highly complicated and conflictual task. Courts in 13 states have established mediation services as an option or requirement for divorcing couples. The state of California, for example, requires mediation for all couples with children under age 12 who have custody and visitation disputes (Pearson et al., 1982).

Private mediation services have proliferated around the country, and a number of practitioners have developed and published model approaches to divorce mediation (e.g., Coogler, 1978; Haynes, 1981; Irving, 1980). Most approaches consist of relatively brief and structured sessions designed to find a solution to a current problem, and seek to promote open, honest, and rationale styles of communication to facilitate the divorce process. The mediator's goals are to aid clients in separating economic and other practical issues from emotional ones and to focus attention on the future. Mediation focuses on the relationships of family members rather than concentrating on one particular person. Parents, children, and other family members may be involved in the mediation sessions. The mediator also maintains a counselor's role and perspective and uses a counseling approach if the need arises. If emotional issues are serious, most mediators refer their clients to other mental health practitioners because the mediator is not a counselor in the traditional sense but merely uses therapeutic techniques to help couples reach a mutually satisfactory agreement (Haynes, 1981).

One of the first mediation organizations was the Family Mediation Association of Atlanta, Georgia, developed by O. J. Coogler in 1975. This private association utilizes principles of conflict resolution and transactional analysis to assist divorcing couples in resolving the conflict surrounding a divorce. Its procedures are representative of most mediation services:

> The first step in mediation is an orientation in which the "Marital Mediation Rules" are explained. If the parties decide to use mediation, they sign a contract with each other and the Association, agreeing to follow the Mediation Rules. The rules provide for the appointment of a mediator and for the couple's selection of an impartial advisory attorney. Secondly, the couple makes a deposit to cover up to 10 hours of mediation time. An additional amount needed for the hours of time expended by the advisory attorney is also deposited. The couple is furnished detailed budget forms to be completed at home as preparation for the first mediation session. At the first mediation session the couple agrees upon arrangements for temporary support and custody so as to stabilize their relationship while they work toward a final settlement. When the couple and the mediator have developed the general form of

the settlement, the advisory attorney is called upon to provide legal and tax advice. The attorney then drafts the formal settlement agreement. Finally, with a legally binding settlement agreement, either party may then obtain an uncontested, "no-fault" divorce at a nominal cost.

Although the husband and wife have signed a contract with a commitment to resolve the issues of their divorce through the mediation process, they are not equally bound to go through with the divorce if they should change their minds. The Family Mediation Association does not promote divorce. Its mediation services are offered to couples who have already decided upon divorce before coming to the Association or have been referred by their therapists when it became apparent divorce was the solution desired.

All communication in mediation is done directly and always in presence of the impartial mediator. Neither husband nor wife is allowed to consult with the mediator privately. Mediators are strictly neutral yet supportive toward both parties. Consequently the husband and wife realize that the mediator will help them avoid having their emotions defeat rationality.

The highly conflictual issues of settlement are discussed and decided on an individual basis. Issues alone are dealt with—not the underlying emotional aspects. It is felt that couples may have difficulty making major decisions about their lives while simultaneously expressing their related feelings. When an emotional issue arises or when someone gets very angry, the mediation process ceases temporarily. The mediator intervenes with the more disturbed party temporarily to resolve the emotional issue while asking the other party to refrain from participating. Afterward the other party will be allowed to express feelings (not respond to the emotional issue) with the first party not responding, only listening. [Coogler et al., 1979: 256-257. Copyrighted 1979 by the National Council on Family Relations, 1910 West County Road B, Suite 147, St. Paul, Minnesota 55113. Reprinted by permission.]

Divorce mediation has been evaluated and found to be superior to adversarial approaches in terms of pretrial agreements, satisfaction with the agreements, reduction in litigation following the divorce, and decrease in public expenses (Sprenkle and Storm, 1983). However, divorce mediation is not without its critics, especially within the legal profession and some women's groups. In these groups, mediation is not regarded as an alternative to more adversarial approaches, but instead a social service that may not adequately represent individuals, especially the less powerful. Such critics complain that:

(1) mediation usually prohibits clients from having legal counsel until the mediation is completed, thus depriving them of knowledge of their legal rights

(2) mediators are not licensed, often not required to complete a specialized course of training, seldom supervised by any public agency, or required to keep current on divorce legislation

(3) mediators have no way of requiring complete and honest disclosure of all the facts necessary in deciding divorce issues

(4) not all parties can honestly and maturely discuss their differences to reach an agreement

(5) mediators cannot protect women from being intimidated by their husbands (Rachofsky, 1985)

Therapeutic Role of Attorneys

Another sign of the legal system's more humanistic approach to divorce is the recognition and legitimization of the divorce attorney's therapeutic role. O'Gorman (1963) conceptualized the attorney role as two basic ideal types: the advocate and the counselor. The advocate represents the traditional stereotype. The advocate is guided by one general principle: to seek maximum benefits for the client within the limits of the law. The advocate focuses on economic issues and deemphasizes emotional and social issues. The counselor type, on the other hand, tries to ascertain the nature of the marital difficulty. She or he takes an active part in uncovering information that may be painful to the client but may lead to a solution that is fair to both parties. The counselor tends to spend more time with a client and often attempts to involve both spouses as well as the attorney for the other spouse. Few attorneys clearly represent this type, but more are demonstrating many of these characteristics as the legal system moves away from an adversarial approach.

Kressel et al. (1978) through in-depth interviews developed another typology of roles played by attorneys in divorce:

(1) *The undertaker* is characterized by a general cynicism and assumes clients are in a state of emotional "derangement;" the lawyer's job is viewed as thankless, messy business.

(2) *The mechanic* is pragmatic, technically oriented, and assumes clients are capable of knowing what they want.

(3) *The mediator* is oriented toward negotiated compromise and rational problem solving with emphasis on cooperation between spouses.

(4) *The social worker* is concerned for clients' postdivorce adjustment and overall social welfare.

(5) *The therapist* assumes legal aspects of a divorce can be handled better if the emotional aspects are also dealt with by the lawyer.

(6) *The moral agent* rejects neutrality and assumes the lawyer should not hesitate to use her or his sense of "right" and "wrong."

Kressel et al. (1978) found many similarities among the roles of therapists, clergy, and attorneys when working with divorcing individuals. The three groups utilized many similar strategies, including reassurance of a favorable outcome, emotional support, empathic listening, and appropriate use of humor and self-disclosure.

To effectively assist a divorcing client in working out a satisfactory agreement, attorneys have found they must first deal with the client's emotional state. For example, Halem (1982) found that 70% of the women and 90% of the men in her sample expressed disappointment and anger over the way their cases were handled by their attorneys. Much of the client dissatisfaction focused on the attorneys' lack of patience, availability, sensitivity, and therapeutic approach. Most attorneys intensely dislike having to deal with the painful emotions of divorcing individuals. Yet in one study two-thirds of the attorneys interviewed admitted playing the counselor role in most, if not all, of their divorce cases, and when asked to offer suggestions for improvement of their role in divorce, attorneys made the following suggestions: (a) formal training in counseling (offered by few law schools), (b) increased knowledge of referral services, and (c) increased sensitivity to the trauma of divorce (Herrman et al., 1979).

The attorney is probably in the most strategic position of all professionals in contact with divorcing families to help clients avoid some of the common problems related to the divorce process. Admittedly, dealing with the client's emotional problems is very stressful for attorneys. Such stress could probably be reduced if the attorneys better understood their clients and knew how to interact with them (Elkin, 1982). This is not to suggest that attorneys become counselors. Rather, selected counseling insights and techniques could facilitate the attorney-client relationship. Also, an understanding of the emotional state of a client should enable an attorney to assess the client's motivation for divorce as well as anticipate and diffuse potential problems in negotiations (Sabalis and Ayers, 1977).

SERVICES FOR CHILDREN

Wallerstein and Kelly (1980) have written the following:

It is a curious phenomenon that family policy in this country has recognized the state's responsibility to offer services in family planning, for prospective children still unborn, but has left parents alone to deal with most of the issues that arise after children are born. Perhaps the time has come for a more realistic family policy, one that addresses the expectable metamorphoses of the American family and the stress points of change. [p. 317]

These authors argue for the availability of help from a neutral counselor or clinician as a necessary adjunct to the process of divorce. Benedek and Benedek (1979) concurred that "while there is certainly substantial divergence as to the nature and amount of assistance required, we believe that all children of divorce are in need of at least some supportive services for some period of time" (p. 157).

The well-documented divorce-related problems that large numbers of children have faced reflect to some extent the inadequacy of services to handle these problems (e.g., McDermott, 1970; Wallerstein and Kelly, 1980). Numerous support services have emerged in recent years to meet the parenting and developmental needs of children involved in divorce, but at present such intervention efforts are uncoordinated, largely experimental, not widely accessible, and lacking systematic evaluation. It must also be acknowledged that several segments of the helping professions have taken responsibility for the welfare of the children of divorce and are moving toward the provision of comprehensive services for these children and their families.

Counseling Approaches

Counseling approaches have been specifically developed for children and their families as they experience divorce. Like counseling for adults, these programs tend to be structured, of limited duration, and crisis-oriented or problem-specific. Also, in this counseling approach, the counselor identifies specific divorce-related problems and develops a treatment program that is intended to resolve them. Such counseling is not intended to effect major personality changes; therefore, it is often insufficient for many children involved in divorce. Some children's problems are such that in-depth therapy is needed where the focus is not only on the feelings that children experience as a result of divorce, but also on particular emotional disturbances such as guilt about anger.

Because children evidence a common pattern of reactions to divorce and are typically in need of emotional support, group approaches have been widely used and deemed highly successful. Like individual counseling, most group approaches are crisis-oriented and time-limited. One exemplary program is the Children of Divorce (COD) groups of Pennsylvania State University (Guerney and Jordan, 1979). This group approach combines education and counseling in a series of six weekly one-hour sessions. The purpose of the group is to provide support for children under stress. It is based on the premise that whether or not children appear to be experiencing particular adjustment problems, they should be provided with therapeutic assistance to try to prevent and/or help resolve personal conflicts stemming from the divorce. Also, the group approach is based on the perspective that while children of divorce require great emotional support and new coping skills, parents are often too preoccupied and emotionally distraught to be of assistance. The primary goals of this group approach are regarded as developmental, not therapeutic, for instance, helping children develop realistic appraisals of their own situation during and following divorce.

Because it has been widely acknowledged by helping professionals that the disruption of parenting is traumatic for children, many counselors and therapists utilize family therapy to facilitate the well-being of children as well as other family members. Typically a standard "loss" model is used to help all family members mourn the loss that the divorce represents so that they may move onward and reorganize family work and activities in a more realistic way (Goldman and Coane, 1977; Hajal and Rosenberg, 1978).

Benedek and Benedek (1979) have described and assessed the various systems for the delivery of counseling services to children and their families. They note that the typical mental health service available to children of divorce is the public child guidance clinic or similar facility. Children and families usually contact these facilities on the advice of family physicians, school officials, or the juvenile court when a problem with a child is recognized. After completion of a conventional evaluation, traditional intervention is initiated, either individual or family therapy. However, the therapy is not usually goal-directed and focuses on problems of daily living rather than problems and feelings related to the divorce. Other avenues for counseling children in divorce are private clinics, therapists in private practice, and experimental programs. With the exception of a few experimental programs, these services tend to be rare, expensive, and are not likely to focus on divorce-related problems and feelings. Experimental programs, in contrast, funded temporarily and serving a small number of clients, provide perhaps the best service to children and parents. These model programs focus specifically upon divorce-related problems and provide goal-directed intervention. They are typically inexpensive, staffed by well-trained and experienced professionals, and systematically evaluated.

Educational Approaches

During the divorce process, a child's sense of continuity and stability is likely to be dependent upon the availability of extrafamilial supports such as the school (Wallerstein and Kelly, 1980). Skeen and McKenry (1980) note the important role that schools can play in facilitating children's adjustment has not been clearly addressed. Because children spend a large number of hours in school, as compared to time with parents, it is reasonable to assume that schools may be providing emotional support and continuity to a large number of children of divorcing parents. Also, many children find some support within the school setting because their attitudes and performance in school provide gratification that is sustaining to them in face of the stress of divorce. Wallerstein and Kelly (1980) found that the attention, sympathy, and tolerance demonstrated by the few teachers who had been informed about the divorce were supportive to a number of children who were feeling emotionally undernourished at home. In their study, some teachers became a central stable figure in the lives of children in the months following parental separation, in some cases the only stable figure in the children's lives. As a result, it has been argued that the school has an obligation to intervene with children of divorce. However, many parents, teachers, and administrators are uncomfortable with the introduction of the subject of divorce either as a part of the curriculum or as a means of therapeutically assisting those children with divorcing parents.

SUMMARY

A wide range of services has become available to divorcing individuals and their families as various helping professionals have responded to the rising rates of divorce. Because of the stigma still attached to divorce and the large numbers of individuals involved, existing helping services are still inadequate. Informal social supports are far more likely to be used than professionals. The counseling profession has been most actively involved in providing assistance through the development and implementation of divorce counseling. However, these counseling techniques have also been adopted by courts, clergy, and attorneys. Divorce mediation has utilized counseling principles to become a viable alternative to the traditional adversarial approach to resolving divorce cases. Children appear to be in particular need of divorce-related support services, yet existing services tend to be in a state of development and not widely available.

REVIEW QUESTIONS

1. Account for the lag by society in providing therapeutic services for divorcing families.
2. How does divorce counseling differ from marriage counseling?
3. Identify and differentiate the various group intervention approaches for divorcing families.

4. How does the role of clergy differ from that of counselors in assisting divorcing individuals and family members?
5. In what ways has the legal system adopted a counseling approach in divorce cases? Account for this overall change in approach to divorce.
6. How does divorce mediation differ from traditional adversarial means of settling divorce cases?
7. What helping services exist for children involved in divorce? Which appear to be the most viable?

SUGGESTED PROJECTS

1. Review the yellow pages in the telephone directory to determine the extent of services in your community that are directed to divorcing individuals and their families.
2. Visit a community mental health center and survey the range of services offered to divorcing individuals and their families.
3. Talk to an attorney about his or her role in divorce. Find out his or her views about divorce mediation, use of counseling techniques in working with clients, compulsory court-related counseling, and major problems in working with divorced individuals and their families.
4. Visit a local bookstore or library and review the many self-help books available for divorcing individuals and their families. What trends are apparent in these books? How useful do you think these books might be?

REFERENCES

ABARBANEL, A. (1979) "Shared parenting after separation and divorce: a study of joint custody." American Journal of Orthopsychiatry 49: 320-329.

ADAMS, B. N. (1986) The Family: A Sociological Interpretation. New York: Harcourt Brace Jovanovich.

AGOPIAN, M. W. (1981) Parental Child-Stealing. Lexington, MA: Lexington Books.

AHRONS, C. R. (1979) "The binuclear family: two households, one family." Alternative Lifestyles 2: 449-515.

AHRONS, C. R. (1980) "Divorce: a crisis of family transition and change." Family Relations 29: 533-540.

AHRONS, C. R. and M. E. BOWMAN (1981) "Changes in family relationships following divorce of an adult child: grandmother's perceptions." Journal of Divorce 5: 49-69.

AHRONS, C. R. and R. H. RODGERS (1987) Divorced Families: A Multidisciplinary, Developmental View. New York: Norton.

AHRONS, C. R. and L. S. WALLISCH (1986) "The relationship between former spouses," in S. Duck and D. Perlman (eds.) Intimate Relationships: Development, Dynamics, and Deterioration. Beverly Hills, CA: Sage.

Alan Guttmacher Institute (1981) Teenage Pregnancy: The Problem That Hasn't Gone Away. New York: Planned Parenthood Federation of America.

ALBRECHT, S. L. (1980) "Reactions and adjustments to divorce: differences in the experiences of males and females." Family Relations 29: 59-69.

ALBRECHT, S. L., H. M. BAHR, and K. L. GOODMAN (1983) Divorce and Remarriage: Problems, Adaptations, and Adjustments. Westport, CT: Greenwood.

ALBRECHT, S. L. and P. R. KUNZ (1980) "The decision to divorce: a social exchange perspective." Journal of Divorce 3: 319-337.

ANSPACH, D. F. (1976) "Kinship and divorce." Journal of Marriage and the Family 38: 323-330.

ANTHONY, E. J. (1974) "Children at risk from divorce: a review," in E. J. Anthony and C. Koupernils (eds.) The Child in His Family. New York: John Wiley.

ARENDELL, T. (1986) Mothers and Divorce: Legal, Economic and Social Dilemmas. Berkeley: University of California Press.

ATKIN, E. and E. RUBIN (1976) Part-Time Fathers. New York: Vanguard.

BANE, M. J. (1976) "Marital disruption and the lives of children." Journal of Social Issues 32: 103-117.

BARDWICK, J. (1971) Psychology of Women: A Study of Biocultural Conflicts. New York: Harper & Row.

BECKER, G. S. (1974) "A theory of marriage," in T. W. Schultz (ed.) Economies of the Family. Chicago: University of Chicago Press.

BECKER, G. S. (1981) A Treatise on the Family. Cambridge: Harvard University Press.

BECKER, G. S., E. M. LANDES, and R. T. MICHAEL (1977) "An economic analysis of marital instability." Journal of Political Economy 85: 141-187.

BELL, R. R. (1979) Marriage and Family Interaction. Homewood, IL: Dorsey.

BEM, S. (1977) Beyond Sex Roles. St. Paul, MN: West.

BENEDEK, R. S. and E. P. BENEDEK (1979) "Children of divorce: can we meet their needs." Journal of Social Issues 35: 155-169.

BERARDO, D. H. (1982) "Divorce and remarriage at middle-age and beyond." Annals of the American Academy of Political and Social Science 464: 132-139.

BERMAN, W. H. (1985) "Continued attachment after legal divorce." Journal of Family Issues 6: 375-392.

BERMAN, W. H. and D. C. TURK (1981) "Adaptation to divorce: problems and coping strategies." Journal of Marriage and the Family 43: 179-189.

BERNARD, J. (1972) The Future of Marriage. New York: World.

BERNARD, A. M. and H. HACKNEY (1983) Untying the Knot: A Guide to Initiating Divorce. Minneapolis, MN: Winston.

BERNSTEIN, B. E. (1977) "Lawyer and counselor as an interdisciplinary team: points for a woman to ponder in considering the basic finances of divorce." Family Coordinator 26: 421-427.

BLACKWELL, R. (1977) The Fighters Guide to Divorce: A No-Holds Barred Strategy for Getting Ahead. Chicago: Henry Regenry.

BLAKE, N. M. (1962) The Road to Reno: A History of Divorce. New York: Macmillan.

BLOCK, M. R., J. L. DAVIDSON, and J. D. GRAMBS (1980) Women Over Forty. New York: Springer.

BLOOD, R. O., Jr. (1962) Marriage. Glencoe, IL: Free Press.

BLOOD, R. O., Jr. and D. M. WOLFE (1960) Husbands and Wives: The Dynamics of Married Living. New York: Free Press.

BLOOM, B. L., S. J. ASHER, and S. W. WHITE (1978) "Marital disruption as a stressor: a review and analysis." Psychological Bulletin 85: 867-894.

BLOOM, B. L. and R. A. CALDWELL (1981) "Sex differences in adjustment during the process of marital separation." Journal of Marriage and the Family 43: 693-701.

BLOOM, B. L. and C. CLEMENT (1984) "Marital sex role orientation and adjustment to separation and divorce." Journal of Divorce 7: 87-98.

BLOOM, B. L. and W. F. HODGES (1981) "The predicament of the newly separated." Community Mental Health Journal 17: 277-293.

BLOOM, B. L., W. F. HODGES, R. A. CALDWELL, L. SYSTLA, and A. R. CEDRONE (1977) "Marital separation: a community survey." Journal of Divorce 1: 7-20.

BLOOM, B. L. and K. R. KINDLE (1985) "Demographic factors in the continuing relationship between former spouses." Family Relations 34: 375-381.

BLOOM, B. L., R. L. NILES, and A. M. TATCHER (1985) "Sources of marital dissatisfaction among newly separated persons." Journal of Family Issues 6: 359-373.

BLOOM, B. L., S. W. WHITE, and S. J. ASHER (1979) "Marital disruption as a stressful life event," in G. Levinger and O. C. Moles (Eds.) Divorce and Separation: Context, Causes, and Consequences. New York: Basic Books.

BOHANNAN, P. (1970) "The six stations of divorce," in P. Bohannan (ed.) Divorce and After. Garden City, NY: Doubleday.

BOOTH, A., D. JOHNSON, and J. N. EDWARDS (1983) "Measuring marital instability." Journal of Marriage and the Family 45: 387-394.

BOULD, S. (1977) "Female-headed families: personal fate control and the provider role." Journal of Marriage and the Family 39: 339-349.

BOWLBY, J. (1969) Attachment and Loss. New York: Basic Books.

BRANDWEIN, R. A., C. A. BROWN, and E. M. FOX (1976) "Women and children last: divorced mothers and their families." Nursing Digest 10: 39-43.

BRANDWEIN, R. A., C. A. BROWN, and E. M. FOX (1974) "Women and children last: the social situation of divorced mothers and their families." Journal of Marriage and the Family 36: 498-514.

BROWN, C. A., R. FELDBERG, E. M. FOX, and J. KOHEN (1976) "Divorce: chance of a new lifetime." Journal of Social Issues 32: 119-133.

BROWN, E. M. (1976) "Divorce counseling," in D. Olson (ed.) Treating Relationships. Lake Mills, IA: Graphic.

BROWN, P. (1976) "Psychological distress and personal growth among women coping with marital dissolution." Ph.D. dissertation. University of Michigan, Ann Arbor.

BROWN, P., D. J. FELTON, V. WHITEMAN, and R. MANELA (1980) "Attachment and distress following marital separation." Journal of Divorce 3: 303-317.

BROWN, P. and H. FOX (1978) "Sex differences in divorce," in E. Gomberg and V. Franks (eds.) Gender and Disordered Behavior: Sex Differences in Psychopathology. New York: Bruner/Mazel.

BROWN, P. and R. MANELA (1977a) "Client satisfaction with marital and divorce counseling." Family Coordinator 26: 294-303.

BROWN, P. and R. MANELA (1977b) "Changing family roles: women and divorce." Journal of Divorce 1: 315-328.

BUEHLER, C. A. and M. J. HOGAN (1980) "Managerial behavior and stress in families headed by divorced women: a proposed framework." Family Relations 29: 525-532.

BUMPASS, L. L. and J. A. SWEET (1972) "Differentials in marital stability." American Sociological Review 37: 754-766.

BURGESS, E. W. and L. S. COTTRELL, Jr. (1939) Predicting Success or Failure in Marriage. Englewood Cliffs, NJ: Prentice-Hall.

BURGESS, E. W. and P. WALLIN (1953) Engagement and Marriage. Philadelphia: J. B. Lippincott.

BURR, W. R. (1976) Successful Marriage: A Principle Approach. Homewood, IL: Dorsey.

CAMPBELL, A., P. E. CONVERSE, and W. L. RODGERS (1976) The Quality of American Life: Perceptions, Evaluations, and Satisfactions. New York: Russell Sage.

CARTER, H. and P. C. GLICK (1976) Marriage and Divorce: A Social and Economic Study. Cambridge, MA: Harvard University Press.

CHAMBERS, T. K. (1979) Making Fathers Pay: The Enforcement of Child Support. Chicago: University of Chicago Press.

CHENG, C. K. and D. S. YAMAMURA (1957) "Interracial marriage and divorce in Hawaii." Social Forces 36: 77-84.

CHERLIN, A. J. (1981) Marriage, Divorce, and Remarriage. Cambridge, MA: Harvard University Press.

CHESTER, R. (1971) "Health and marriage breakdown: experience of a sample of divorced women." British Journal of Preventive and Social Medicine 25: 231-235.

CHESTER, R. (1977) Divorce in Europe. Leiden, Netherlands: Martinus Nijhoff.

"The Children of Divorce." (February, 1980) Newsweek, pp. 58-66.

CHIRIBOGA, D. A. (1979) "Marital separation and stress." Alternative Lifestyles 2: 461-470.

CHIRIBOGA, D. A. (1982) "Adaptation to marital separation in later and earlier life." Journal of Gerontology 1: 109-114.

CHIRIBOGA, D. A., A. COHO, J. A. STEIN, and J. ROBERTS (1979) "Divorce, stress, and social supports: a study in help-seeking behavior." Journal of Divorce 3: 121-135.

CHIRIBOGA, D. A. and L. CUTLER (1978) "Stress responses among divorcing men and women." Journal of Divorce 2: 21-36.

CHIRIBOGA, D. A., J. ROBERTS, and J. A. STEIN (1978) "Psychological well-being during marital separation." Journal of Divorce 2: 21-36.

CHIRIBOGA, D. A. and M. THURNHER (1980) "Marital lifestyles and adjustment to separation." Journal of Divorce 3: 379-390.

CLARK, H. (1968) The Law of Domestic Relations in the United States. St. Paul: West.

CLEVELAND, M. (1979) "Divorce in the middle years: The sexual dimension." Journal of Divorce 2: 255-262.

CLINE, D. and J. WESTMAN (1971) "The impact of divorce on the family." Child Psychiatry and Human Development 2: 78-83.

COMBS, E. R. (1979) "The human capital concept as a basis for property settlement at divorce." Journal of Divorce 2: 329-356.

"Congress Sends Reagan Child Support Measure." (August 11, 1984) Congressional Quarterly, pp. 1965-1966.

COOGLER, O. J. (1978) Structured Mediation in Divorce Settlements. Lexington, MA: D. C. Heath.

COOGLER, O. J., R. E. WEBER, and P. C. McKENRY (1979) "Divorce mediation: a means of facilitating divorce and adjustment." Family Coordinator 28: 255-259.

COOMBS, L. C. and Z. ZUMETA (1970) "Correlates of marital dissolution in a prospective fertility study: a research note." Social Problems 18: 92-101.

CORCORAN, M. (1979) "The economic consequences of marital dissolution for women in the middle years." Sex Roles 5: 343-353.

CROSBY, J. F. (1980) "A critique of divorce statistics and their interpretation." Family Relations 29: 51-58.

CUBER, J. F. and P. B. HARROFF (1965) Sex and the Significant Americans: A Study of Sexual Behavior Among the Affluent. New York: Appleton-Century.

CUTRIGHT, P. (1971) "Income family events. Marital stability." Journal of Marriage and the Family 33: 291-306.

DeFRAIN, J. and R. EIRICK (1981) "Coping as divorced single parents: a comparative study of fathers and mothers." Family Relations 30: 265-274.

DEMOS, J. (1975) "Myths and realities in the history of American life," in H. Gruenbaum and J. Christ (eds.) Contemporary Marriage: Structure, Dynamics, and Therapy. Boston: Little, Brown.

DERDEYN, A. P. (1976) "Child custody contests in historical perspective." American Journal of Psychiatry 133: 1369-1375.

DeSHANE, M. R. and K. BROWN-WILSON (1981) "Divorce in late life: a call for research." Journal of Divorce 4: 81-91.

DESPERT, J. (1962) Children of Divorce. Garden City, NY: Dolphin.

DIXON, R. B., and L. J. WEITZMAN (1980) "Evaluating the impact of no-fault divorce in California." Family Relations 29: 297-307.

DIXON, R. B. and L. J. WEITZMAN (1982) "When husbands file for divorce." Journal of Marriage and the Family 44: 103-115.

DREYFUS, E. A. (1979) "Counseling the divorced father." Journal of Marital and Family Therapy 5: 79-82.

DYER, E. D. (1983) Courtship, Marriage, and Family: American Style. Homewood, IL: Dorsey.

EDEN, P. (1979) "How inflation flaunts the court's orders." Family Advocate 1: 2-5.

EDWARDS, C. S. (1985) "Updated estimates of the cost of raising a child." Family Economics Review 4:26.

EISLER, R. T. (1977) Dissolution: No-Fault Divorce, Marriage, and the Future of Women. New York: McGraw-Hill.

ELKIN, M. (1977) "Postdivorce counseling in a conciliation court." Journal of Divorce 1: 55-65.

ELKIN, M. (1982) "The missing links in divorce law: a redefinition of process and practice." Journal of Divorce 6: 37-63.

ENGLAND, J. L. and P. R. KUNZ (1975) "The application of age-specific rates to divorce." Journal of Marriage and the Family 31: 40-46.

ESHLEMAN, J. R. (1985) The Family: An Introduction. Boston: Allyn & Bacon.

ESMAN, A. H. (1971) "Happy marriage and its effects on children." Medical Aspects of Human Sexuality 5: 37-47.

ESPENSHADE, T. (1979) "The economic consequences of divorce." Journal of Marriage and the Family 41: 615-625.

FAIN, H. M. (1977) "Family law—'whither now?'" Journal of Divorce 1: 31-42.

FEDERICO, J. (1979) "The marital termination period of the divorce adjustment process." Journal of Divorce 3: 93-106.

FENELON, B. (1971) "State variations in United States divorce rates." Journal of Marriage and the Family 27: 321-327.

FELD, A. L. (1976) "Divorce tax style." Taxes 54: 608-612.

FISHER, E. O. (1974) Divorce—The New Freedom: A Guide to Divorcing and Divorce Counseling. New York: Harper & Row.

FLYNN, C. (1987) "Rethinking joint custody policy: option or presumption." Unpublished manuscript available from the author, Department of Child Development and Family Relations, University of North Carolina, Greensboro.

"For divorce, a revolution in the courtroom." (February 7, 1983) New York Times, p. A14.

FREED, D. J. and T. B. WALKER (1986) "Family law in the fifty states: an overview." Family Law Quarterly 19: 331-441.

FRIEDMAN, H. J. (1980) "The father's parenting experience in divorce." American Journal of Orthopsychiatry 137: 1177-1182.

FROILAND, D. J. and T. L. HOZMAN (1977) "Counseling for constructive divorce." Personnel and Guidance Journal 55: 525-529.

FURSTENBERG, F. (1976) "Premarital pregnancy and marital instability." Journal of Social Issues 32: 67-86.

FURSTENBERG, F. A. and C. W. NORD (1985) "Parenting apart: patterns of child rearing after marital disruption." Journal of Marriage and the Family 47: 893-904.

GALLIGAN, R. J. and S. J. BAHR (1978) "Economic well-being and marital stability: implications for income maintenance programs." Journal of Marriage and the Family 40: 283-290.

GARDNER, R. A. (1982) "Joint custody is not for everyone." Family Advocate 5: 7-9, 45-46.

GEERKIN, M. and W. R. GOVE (1974) "Race, sex, and marital status: their effect on mortality." Social Problems 21: 567-580.

GELLES, R. J. (1984) "Parental child snatching: a preliminary estimate of national incidence." Journal of Marriage and the Family 46: 735-739.

GETTLEMAN, S. and J. MARKOWITZ (1974) The Courage to Divorce. New York: Simon & Schuster.

GLENN, N. D. and M. SUSPANIC (1984) "The social and demographic correlates of divorce and separation in the United States: an update and reconsideration." Journal of Marriage and the Family 46: 563-575.

GLENN, N. D. and B. S. SHELTON (1985) "Regional differences in divorce in the United States." Journal of Marriage and the Family 47: 641-652.

GLICK, P. C. (1977) "Updating the life cycle of the family." Journal of Marriage and the Family 39: 5-14.

GLICK, P. C. (1979) "Children of divorced parents in demographic perspective." Journal of Social Issues 35: 170-182.

GLICK, P. C. (1984) "Marriage, divorce, and living arrangements." Journal of Family Issues 5: 7-26.

GLICK, P. C. (1986) "Recent changes in divorce and remarriage." Journal of Marriage and the Family 48: 737-747.

GLICK, P. and A. NORTON (1977) "Marrying, divorcing, and living together in the U. S. today." Population Bulletin 32: 2-39.

GLICK, P. C. and A. NORTON (1980) "New lifestyles change family statistics." American Demographics 2: 20-23.

GOETTING, A. (1979) "The normative integration of the former spouse relationship." Journal of Divorce 2: 395-414.

GOETTING, A. (1981) "Divorce outcome research: issues and perspectives." Journal of Family Issues 2: 350-378.

GOETTING, A. (1982) "The six stations of remarriage: developmental tasks of remarriage after divorce." Family Relations 31: 213-222.

GOLDMAN, J. and J. COANE (1977) "Family therapy after divorce: developing a strategy." Family Process 16: 357-362.

GOLDSMITH, J. (1980) "Relationships between former spouses: descriptive findings." Journal of Divorce 4: 1-20.

GOODE, W. J. (1956) After Divorce. New York: Free Press.

GOODE, W. J. (1963) World Revolution and Family Patterns. New York: Free Press.

GOVE, W. R. (1973) "Sex, marital status, and mortality." American Journal of Sociology 79: 45-67.

GRANVOLD, D. K. (1983) "Structured separation for marital treatment and decision-making." Journal of Marital and Family Therapy 9: 403-412.

GRANVOLD, D. K., L. M. PEDLER, and S. G. SCHEILLIC (1979) "A study of sex role expectancy and female postdivorce adjustment." Journal of Divorce 2: 383-393.

GRANVOLD, D. K. and G. J. WELCH (1977) "Intervention for post-divorce adjustment problems: the treatment seminar." Journal of Divorce 1: 81-92.

GRAY, G. M. (1978) "The nature of the psychological impact of divorce upon the individual." Journal of Divorce 1: 289-301.

GREEN, R. G. and M. J. SPORAKOWSKI (1983) "The dynamics of divorce: marital quality, alternative attractions, and external pressures." Journal of Divorce 7: 77-88.

GUBRIUM, J. F. (1974) "Marital desolation and the evaluation of everyday life in old age." Journal of Marriage and the Family 36: 107-113.

GUERNEY, L. and L. JORDAN (1979) "Children of divorce: a community support group." Journal of Divorce 2: 283-294.

GUNTER, B. C. (1977) "Notes on divorce filing as role behavior." Journal of Marriage and the Family 39: 95-98.

GUNTER, B. G. and D. P. JOHNSON (1978) "Divorce filing as role behavior: effect of no-fault law on divorce filing pattern." Journal of Marriage and the Family 40: 571-574.

HAJAL, F. and E. B. ROSENBERG (1978) "Working with the one-parent family in family therapy." Journal of Divorce 1: 259-269.

HALEM, L. C. (1982) Separated and Divorced Women. New York: Greenwood.

HANNAN, M. T., N. B. TUMA, and L. P. GROENEVELD (1978) "Income and independence effects on a marital dissolution: results from the Seattle and Denver income-maintenance experiments." American Journal of Sociology 84: 611-633.

HARMELINK, P. J. and N. E. SHURTZ (1977) "Tax effects in divorce planning." CPA Journal 47: 27-32.

HAYNES, J. M. (1981) Divorce and Mediation: A Practical Guide for Therapists and Counselors. New York: Springer.

HERMANN, S. J. (1974) "Divorce: a grief process." Perspectives in Psychiatric Care 12: 108-112.

HERRMAN, M. S., P. C. McKENRY, and R. E. WEBER (1979) "Attorneys' perceptions of their role in divorce." Journal of Divorce 2: 313-322.

HERZOG, E. and C. E. SUDIA (1971) Boys in Fatherless Families. Washington, DC: Government Printing Office.

HESS, R. D. and K. A. CAMARA (1979) "Post-divorce family relationships as mediating factors in the consequences of divorce for children." Journal of Social Issues 35: 79-96.

HETHERINGTON, E. M. (1979) "Divorce: a child's perspective." American Psychologist 34: 851-858.

HETHERINGTON, E. M., M. COX, and R. COX (1976) "Divorced fathers." Family Coordinator 25: 417-428.

HETHERINGTON, E. M., M. COX, and R. COX (1978) "The aftermath of divorce," in J. H. Stevens and M. Matthews (eds.) Mother-Child, Father-Child Relations. Washington, DC: National Association for the Education of Young Children.

HETHERINGTON, E. M., M. COX, and R. COX (1979a) "The development of children in mother-headed families," in H. Hoffman and D. Reiss (eds.) The American Family: Dying or Developing. New York: Plenum.

HETHERINGTON, E. M., M. COX, and R. COX (1979b) "Family interactions and the social emotional and cognitive development of children following divorce," in V. C. Vaughan and T. B. Brazleton (eds.) The Family: Setting Priorities. New York: Science and Medicine.

HETHERINGTON, E. M., M. COX, and R. COX (1979c) "Stress and coping in divorce: a focus on women," in J. Gullahorn (ed.) Psychology and Women in Transition. New York: B. J. Winston.

HETHERINGTON, E. M., M. COX, and R. COX (1985) "Long-term effects of divorce and remarriage on the adjustment of children." Journal of Child Psychiatry 56: 518-530.

HETHERINGTON, E. M. and R. D. PARKE (1979) Child Psychology: A Contemporary Viewpoint. New York: McGraw-Hill.

HICKS, M. W. and M. PLATT (1970) "Marital happiness and stability: a review of the research in the sixties." Journal of Marriage and the Family 32: 553-573.

HILL, R. (1949) Families Under Stress. New York: Harper & Row.

HODGES, W. F., R. C. WECHSLER, and C. BALLENTINE (1979) "Divorce and the preschool child: cumulative stress." Journal of Divorce 3: 55-67.

HOLMES, T. and R. RAHE (1976) "The social readjustment rating scale." Journal of Psychosomatic Research 11: 213-218.

HONIG, M. (1973) "The impact of welfare levels on family stability," in Joint Economic Committee (ed.) "The family, poverty, and welfare programs: factors influencing family instability," Studies in Public Welfare No. 12, Part 1. Washington, DC: Government Printing Office.

HOUSEKNECHT, S. K. and G. B. SPANIER (1980) "Marital disruption and higher education among women in the United States." Sociological Quarterly 21: 375-389.

HOZMAN, T. L. and D. J. FROILAND (1977) "Children forgotten in divorce." Personnel and Guidance Journal 55: 530-533.

HUBER, J. and G. SPITZE (1980) "Considering divorce: an expansion of Becker's theory of marital instability." American Journal of Sociology 86: 75-89.

HUNT, M. (1966) The World of the Formerly Married. New York: McGraw-Hill.

HUNT, M. (1974) Sexual Behavior in the 1970s. Chicago: Playboy.

HUNT, M. and B. HUNT (1977) The Divorce Experience. New York: McGraw-Hill.

HUTTER, M. (1981) The Changing Family: Comparative Perspectives. New York: John Wiley.

HYNES, W. J. (1979) "Single parent mothers and distress: relationships between selected social and psychological factors and distress in low-income single parent mothers." Ph.D. dissertation. Catholic University of America, Washington, D.C.

IRVING, H. H. (1980) Divorce Mediation: A Rational Alternative to the Adversary System. New York: Universe.

JACOBSON, D. S. (1978) "The impact of marital separation/divorce on children: II. parent-child separation and child adjustment." Journal of Divorce 1: 341-360.

JOHNSON, E. S. and B. H. VINICK (1981) "Support of the parent when an adult son or daughter divorces." Journal of Divorce 5: 69-79.

JOHNSON, M. P. (1985) "Commitment, cohesion, investment barriers, alternatives, constraint: why do people stay together when they really don't want to ." Presented at the Theory Construction and Research Methodology Workshop, National Council on Family Relations Annual Meeting, Dallas, TX.

JOHNSON, W. D. (1976) "The economic ramifications of divorce preparation through counseling." Conciliation Courts Review 14: 37-42.

JONES, F. N. (1977) "The impact of divorce on children." Conciliation Courts Review 15: 25-29.

JUHASY, A. M. (1979) "A concept for divorce: not busted bond but severed strand." Alternative Lifestyles 2: 471-482.

KASLOW, F. (1984) "Divorce: an evolutionary process of change in the family system." Journal of Divorce 7: 21-39.

KASLOW, F. and R. HYATT (1981) "Divorce: a potential growth experience for the extended family." Journal of Divorce 5: 115-126.

KEPHART, W. M. (1981) The Family, Society, and the Individual. Boston: Houghton Mifflin.

KESSLER, S. (1975) The American Way of Divorce: Prescriptions for Change. Chicago: Nelson Hall.

KESSLER, S. (1978) "Building skills in divorce adjustment groups." Journal of Divorce 2: 209-215.

KIMURA, Y. (1957) "War brides in Hawaii and their in-laws." American Journal of Sociology 63: 70-76.

KITSON, G. C. (1985) "Marital discord and marital separation: a county survey." Journal of Marriage and the Family 47: 693-700.

KITSON, G. C., W. M. HOLMES, and M. B. SUSSMAN (1983) "Withdrawing divorce petitions: predictive test of the exchange model of divorce." Journal of Divorce 7: 51-66.

KITSON, G. C. (1982) "Attachment to the spouse in divorce: a scale and its application." Journal of Marriage and the Family 44: 379-393.

KITSON, G. C. and J. K. LANGLIE (1984) "Couples who file for divorce but change their minds." American Journal of Orthopsychiatry 54: 469-489.

KITSON, G. C., R. N. MOIR, and P. R. MASON (1982) "Family social support in crises: the special case of divorce." American Journal of Orthopsychiatry 52: 161-165.

KITSON, G. C. and H. J. RASCHKE (1981) "Divorce research: what we know; what we need to know." Journal of Divorce 4: 1-37.

KITSON, G. C. and M. SUSSMAN (1982) "Marital complaints, demographic character-istics and symptoms of mental distress in divorce." Journal of Marriage and the Family 44: 87-101.

KOHEN, J. A., C. A. BROWN, and R. FELDBERG (1979) "Divorced mothers: the costs and benefits of female family control," in G. Levinger and O. C. Moles (eds.) Divorce and Separation. New York: Basic Books.

KRANTZLER, M. (1973) Creative Divorce: A New Opportunity for Personal Growth. New York: M. Evans.

KRAUS, S. (1979) "The crisis of divorce: growth promoting or pathogenic." Journal of Divorce: 107-119.

KRESSEL, K. and M. DEUTSCH (1977) "Divorce therapy: an in-depth survey of therapists' views." Family Process 16: 413-443.

KRESSEL, K., N. JAFFE, B. TACHMAN, C. WATSON, and M. DEUTSCH (1980) "A typology of divorcing couples: implications for mediation and the divorce process." Family Process 19: 101-116.

KRESSEL, K., M. LOPEZ-MORILLAS, J. WEINGLASS, and M. DEUTSCH (1978) "Professional interventions in divorce: a summary of the views of lawyers, psychotherapists, and clergy." Journal of Divorce 2: 119-155.

KRESSEL, L. (1980) "Patterns of coping in divorce and some implications for clinical practice." Family Relations 29: 234-240.

KUBLER-ROSS, E. (1969) On Death and Dying. New York: Macmillan.

KURDEK, L. A., D. BLISK, and A. E. SIESKY (1981) "Correlates of children's long-term adjustment to their parents' divorce." Developmental Psychology 5: 565-579.

KURDEK, L. A. and A. E. SIESKY (1980) "Children's perceptions of their parents' divorce." Journal of Divorce 3: 339-378.

KURTZ, P. M. (1977) "The state equal rights amendments and their impact on domestic relations law." Family Law 11: 101-150.

LADBROOK, D. (1976) "The health and survival of the divorced." Conciliation Courts Review 14: 21-33.

LANDIS, J. T. (1960) "The trauma of children when parents divorce." Marriage and Family Living 22: 7-13.

LANDIS, J. T. (1963) "Social correlates of divorce or nondivorce among the unhappily married." Marriage and Family Living 25: 178-180.

LANGELIER, R. and P. DECKERT (1980) "Divorce counseling guidelines for the late divorced female." Journal of Divorce 3: 403-411.

LASCH, C. (1973) The World of Nations. New York: Knopf.

LAVOIE, R. (November, 1978) "Who gets what in a divorce?" Money, pp. 66-69.

LERNER, M. (1957) America as a Civilization. New York: Simon & Schuster.

LESLIE, G. (1982) The Family in Social Context. New York: Oxford University Press.

LESLIE, G. R. and S. K. KORMAN (1985) The Family in Social Context. New York: Oxford University Press.

LESLIE, G. R. and E. M. LESLIE (1980) Marriage in a Changing World. New York: John Wiley.

LEVINGER, G. (1965) "Marital cohesiveness and dissolution: an integrative review." Journal of Marriage and the Family 27: 19-28.

LEVINGER, G. (1966) "Sources of marital dissatisfaction among applicants for divorce." American Journal of Orthopsychiatry 36: 803-807.

LEVINGER, G. (1979a) "A social psychological perspective on marital dissolution," in G. Levinger and O. C. Moles (eds.) Divorce and Separation: Context, Causes, and Consequences. New York: Basic Books.

LEVINGER, G. (1979b) "Marital cohesiveness at the brink: the fate of applications for divorce," in G. Levinger and O. C. Moles (eds.) Divorce and Separation: Context, Causes, and Consequences. New York: Basic Books.

LEVY, T. M. and W. JOFFE (1978) "Counseling couples through separation: a developmental approach." Family Therapy 5: 267-276.

LEWIS, R. A. and G. B. SPANIER (1979) "Theorizing about the quality and stability of marriage," in W. R. Burr et al. (eds.) Contemporary Theories About the Family. New York: Free Press.

LOCKE, H. J. (1951) Predicting Adjustment in Marriage: A Comparison of a Divorced and a Happily Married Group. New York: Holt.

LONGFELLOW, C. (1979) "Divorce in context: its impact on children," in G. Levinger and O. C. Moles (eds.) Divorce and Separation: Context, Causes, and Consequences. New York: Basic Books.

LOWENTHAL, M. C., M. THURNHER, and D. CHIRIBOGA (1975) "Four stages of life: a comparative study of women and men facing transitions. San Francisco: Jossey-Bass.

LOWERY, C. R. and S. A. SETTLE (1985) "Effects of divorce on children: differential impact of custody and visitation patterns." Family Relations 34: 455-463.

LUCKEY, E. (1964) "Marital satisfaction and personality correlates of spouse." Journal of Marriage and the Family 26: 217-220.

LUEPNITZ, D. A. (1982) Child Custody. Lexington, MA: Lexington.

LYNCH, J. J. (1977) The Broken Heart: The Medical Consequences of Loneliness. New York: Basic Books.

MAGRAB, P. R. (1978) "For the sake of the children: a review of the psychological effects of divorce." Journal of Divorce 3: 233-245.

McCUBBIN, H. and B. B. DAHL (1985) Marriage and Family: Individuals and Life Cycles. New York: John Wiley.

McDERMOTT, J. F. (1968) "Parental divorce in early childhood." American Journal of Psychiatry 10: 1424-1432.

McDERMOTT, J. F. (1970) "Divorce and its psychiatric sequelae in children." Archives of General Psychiatry 23: 421-427.

MEAD, M. (1971) "Anomalies in American postdivorce relationships," in P. Bohannan (ed.) Divorce and After. New York: Anchor.

MELICHAR, J. and D. A. CHIRIBOGA (1985) "Timetables in the divorce process." Journal of Marriage and the Family 47: 701-708.

MENAGHAN, E. G. (1985) "Depressive affect and subsequent divorce." Journal of Family Issues 6: 295-306.

MENDES, H. A. (1976) "Single fathers." Family Coordinator 25: 439-444.

MILLER, M. H. (1971) "A comparison of the duration of interracial with intraracial marriages in Hawaii." International Journal of Sociology of the Family 1: 197-201.

MINUCHIN, S. (1974) Families and Family Therapy. Cambridge, MA: Harvard University Press.

MITCHELL, K. (1983) "The price tag of responsibility: a comparison of divorced and remarried mothers." Journal of Divorce 6: 33-41.

MOLLER, A. S. (1975) "Jewish-Gentile divorce in California." Jewish Social Studies 37: 275-290.

MONAHAN, T. P. (1962) "When married couples part: statistical trends and relationships in divorce." American Sociological Review 27: 625-633.

MONAHAN, T. P. (1970) "Are interracial marriages really less stable?" Social Forces 1954, 48: 461-473.

MORELAND, J. and A. SCHWEBEL (1981) "A gender role transcendent perspective on fathering." Counseling Psychologist 9: 45-54.

MORELAND, J., A. I. SCHWEBEL, M. A. FINE, and J. D. VESS (1982) "Post-divorce family therapy: suggestions for professionals." Professional Psychology 13: 639-646.

MOTT, F. L. and S. F. MOORE (1977) "Marital disruption: causes and consequences," in F. L. Mott et al. (eds.) Years for Decision, Vol. 4. Columbus, OH: Ohio State University, Center for Human Resources Research.

MOTT, F. L. and S. F. MOORE (1979) "The course of marital disruption among young American women: an interdisciplinary perspective." Journal of Marriage and the Family 41: 355-356.

MUELLER, C. W. and H. POPE (1977) "Marital instability: a study of its transmission between generations." Journal of Marriage and the Family 39: 83-93.

MURDOCK, G. P. (1950) "Family stability in non-European cultures." Annals of the American Academy of Political and Social Science 272: 195-201.

MURSTEIN, B. and V. GLAUDIN (1968) "The relationship of marital adjustment to personality: a factor analysis of the interpersonal check list." Journal of Marriage and the Family 30: 651-655.

MYERS, J. C. (1976) "The adjustment of women to marital separation: the affects of sex-role identification and of stage in family life, as determined by age and presence or absence of dependent children." Ph.D. dissertation. University of Colorado, Boulder.

National Center for Health Statistics (1970) "Mortality from selected causes by marital status," Series 20, No. 8A. Washington, DC: Government Printing Office.

National Center for Health Statistics (July 19, 1985) "Births, marriages, divorces, and deaths for May 1984," Monthly Vital Statistics Report. Washington, DC: Department of Health and Human Services.

National Center for Health Statistics (September 25, 1986) Monthly Vital Statistics Report. Washington, DC: Department of Health and Human Services.

NELSON, G. (1981) "Moderators of women's and children adjustment following parental divorce." Journal of Divorce 4: 71-83.

NORTON, A. J. and P. C. GLICK (1976) "Marital instability: past, present and future." Journal of Social Issues 32: 5-20.

NORTON, A. J. and P. C. GLICK (1986) "One parent families: a social and economic profile." Family Relations 35: 9-17.

NORTON, A. J. and J. E. MOORMAN (1987) "Current trends in marriage and divorce among American women." Journal of Marriage and the Family 49: 3-14.

NYE, F. I. (1957) "Child adjustment in broken and in unhappy unbroken homes." Marriage and Family Living 19: 356-361.

NYE, F. I. and F. M. BERARDO (1973) The Family: Its Structure and Interaction. New York: Macmillan.

OAKLAND, T. (1984) Divorced Fathers: Reconstructing a Quality Life. New York: Human Sciences.

O'GORMAN, H. J. (1963) Lawyers in Matrimonial Cases. New York: Free Press.

"One-fifth of America's children now live in single-parent families." (August, 1982) Marriage and Divorce Today: 2-3.

ORTHNER, D., T. BROWN, and D. FERGUSON (1976) "Single parent fatherhood: an emerging lifestyle." Family Coordinator 25: 429-438.

PAIS, J. and P. WHITE (1979) "Family redefinition: a review of the literature toward a model of divorce adjustment." Journal of Divorce 2: 271-281.

PARKES, C. M. (1973) "Separation anxiety: an aspect of the search for a lost object," in R. S. Weiss (ed.) Loneliness: The Experience of Emotional and Social Isolation. Cambridge: MIT Press.

PEARLIN, L. I. and J. S. JOHNSON (1977) "Marital status, life strains and depression." American Sociological Review 42: 704-715.

PEARLIN, L. I. and C. SCHOOLER (1978) "The structure of coping." Journal of Health and Social Behavior 19: 2-21.

PEARSON, J., N. THONNES, and L. VANDERKOOI (1982) "The decision to mediate: profiles of individuals who accept and reject the opportunity to mediate contested child custody and visitation issues." Journal of Divorce 6: 17-35.

PETT, M. G. (1982) "Predictors of satisfactory social adjustment of divorced single parents." Journal of Divorce 5: 1-17.

POPE, H. and C. W. MUELLER (1979) "The intergenerational transmission of marital instability," in G. Levinger and O. C. Moles (eds.) Divorce and Separation: Context, Causes, and Consequences. New York: Basic Books.

PRICE-BONHAM, S. and J. O. BALSWICK (1980) "The noninstitutions: divorce, desertion, and remarriage." Journal of Marriage and the Family 42: 225-238.

PRICE-BONHAM, S. and J. M. BONHAM (1982) "Child support: a proposal." Unpublished manuscript.

PRICE-BONHAM, S., D. WRIGHT, and J. PITTMAN (1982) "Former spouse relationships: a typology." Presented at the Annual Meeting of the World Congress of Sociology, Mexico City, Mexico.

RACHOFSKY, M. (1985) "Settling for less: experience shows divorce mediation is hostile to women." Guild Notes (Winter): 6.

RASCHKE, H. (1987) "Divorce," in M. Sussman and S. Steinmetz (eds.) Handbook of Marriage and the Family. New York: Plenum.

RASCHKE, H. J. (1979) "Social-psychological consequences of divorce: a comparison of Black and White low-income single parent families." Presented at the Annual Meeting of the American Sociological Association, Boston.

RASCHKE, H. J. and K. D. BARRINGER (1977) "Postdivorce adjustment among persons participating in Parents Without Partners organizations." Family Perspective 11:23-34.

RASCHKE, H. J. and E. MARRONI (1977) "Adjustment to marital dissolution." Presented at the Annual Meeting of the Society for the Study of Social Problems, San Francisco.

RASCHKE, H. J. and V. J. RASCHKE (1979) "Family conflict and children's self-concepts: a comparison of intact and single-parent families." Journal of Marriage and the Family 41: 367-374.

RENNE, K. (1971) "Health and marital experiences in an urban population." Journal of Marriage and the Family 33: 338-350.

RHEINSTEIN, M. (1972) Marriage Stability, Divorce, and the Law. Chicago: University of Chicago Press.

RICE, D. G. (1977) "Psychotherapeutic treatment of narcissistic injury in marital separation and divorce." Journal of Divorce 1: 119-128.

RICE, D. G. (1979) Dual-Career Marriage. New York: Free Press.

RISMAN, B. J. (1986) "Can men 'mother'? Life as a single father." Family Relations 35: 95-102.

ROBERTS, T. W. and S. J. PRICE (1985/86) "A systems analysis of the remarriage process: implications for the clinician." Journal of Divorce 9: 1-25.

ROBERTSON, N. (1975) "Divorce around the world: even when easy, it carries a stigma." New York Times.

ROSE, V. L. and S. PRICE-BONHAM (1973) "Divorce adjustment: a woman's problem?" Family Coordinator 22: 291-297.

ROSS, H. and V. SAWHILL (1975) Time of Transition: The Growth of Families Headed by Women. Washington, DC: Urban Institute.

RUTTER, M. (1971) "Parent-child separations: psychological effects on the children." Journal of Child Psychology and Psychiatry 12: 233-260.

SABALIS, R. F. and G. W. AYERS (1977) "Emotional aspects of divorce and their effects on the legal process." Family Coordinator 26: 391-394.

SALTS, C. J. (1979) "Divorce process: integrating theory." Journal of Divorce 2: 233-240.

SALTS, C. J. and C. E. ZONGKER (1983) "Effects of divorce counseling groups on adjustment and self-concept." Journal of Divorce 6: 55-67.

SANTROCK, J. W. and R. A. WARSHAK (1979) "Father custody and social development in boys and girls." Journal of Social Issues 35: 112-125.

SAWHILL, I. V. (1975) "Discrimination and poverty among women who head families." Presented at Conference on Occupational Segregation, Wellsley College.

SCANZONI, J. (1979) "A historical perspective on husband-wife bargaining, power, and marital dissolution," in G. K. Levinger and O. C. Moles (eds.) Divorce and Separation: Context, Causes, and Consequences. New York: Basic Books.

SCANZONI, J. and M. SZINOVACZ (1980) Family Decision Making: A Developmental Sex Role Model. Beverly Hills, CA: Sage.

SCHULMAN, G. L. (1981) "Divorce, single parenthood, and stepfamilies: Structural implications of the transactions." International Journal of Family Therapy: 87-112.

SEAGULL, A. A. and E. A. SEAGULL (1977) "The non-custodial father's relationship to his child: conflicts and solutions." Journal of Clinical Child Psychology 6: 11-15.

SEAL, K. (1979) "A decade of no-fault divorce: what it has meant financially for women in California." Family Advocate 1: 10-15.

SHIELDS, L. (1981) Displaced Homemakers. New York: McGraw-Hill.

SKEEN, P. and P. C. McKENRY (1980) "The teacher's role in facilitating a child's adjustment to divorce." Young Children 35: 3-12.

SMART, L. S. (1979) "An application of Erickson's theory to the recovery-from-divorce process." Journal of Divorce 1: 67-79.

SMITH, C. E. (1966) "The Negro-White intermarriage: forbidden sexual union." Journal of Sex Research 2: 169-173.

SMITH, J. S. and E. S. BENINGER (1982) "Women's nonmarket labor: dissolution of marriage and opportunity cost." Journal of Family Issues 3: 251-265.

SONNE, J. C. (1974) "On the question of compulsory marriage counseling as a part of divorce proceedings." Family Coordinator 23: 303-305.

SORENSEN, A. and M. McDONALD (1982) "Does child support support the children." Children and Youth Services Review 4: 53-66.

SOUTH, S. J. and G. SPITZE (1986) "Determinants of divorce over the marital life course." American Sociological Review 51: 583-590.

SPANIER, G. B. and E. A. ANDERSON (1979) "The impact of the legal system on adjustment to marital separation." Journal of Marriage and the Family 41: 605-613.

SPANIER, G. B., and CASTO, R. F. (1979) "Adjustment to separation and divorce: an analysis of 50 case studies." Journal of Divorce 2: 241-253.

SPANIER, G. B. and S. HANSON (1981) "The role of extended kin in the adjustment to marital separation." Journal of Divorce 5: 33-48.

SPANIER, G. B. and P. C. GLICK (1980) "Paths to remarriage." Journal of Divorce 3: 283-296.

SPANIER, G. B. and M. E. LACHMAN (1979) "Factors associated with adjustment to marital separation." Presented at the Annual Meeting of the Eastern Sociological Society, New York.

SPANIER, G. B. and R. LEWIS (1980) "Marital quality: a review of the seventies." Journal of Marriage and the Family 42: 825-840.

SPANIER, G. and L. THOMPSON (1983) "Relief and distress after marital separation." Journal of Divorce 7: 31-49.

SPANIER, G. and L. THOMPSON (1984) "Parting: the aftermath of separation and divorce." Beverly Hills, CA: Sage.

SPICER, J. W. and G. D. HAMPE (1975) "Kinship interaction after divorce." Journal of Marriage and the Family 37: 113-149.

SPITZE, G. and J. SOUTH (1985) "Women's employment, time expenditure, and divorce." Journal of Family Issues 6: 307-329.

SPRENKLE, D. H. and C. L. STORM (1983) "Divorce therapy outcome research: a substantive and methodological review." Journal of Marital and Family Therapy 9: 239-258.

STACK, S. (1980) "The effects of marital dissolution on suicide." Journal of Marriage and the Family 42: 83-92.

STEINMAN, S. (1981) "The experience of children in a joint-custody arrangement: a report of a study." American Journal of Orthopsychiatry 51: 403-414.

STETSON, D. M. and G. C. WRIGHT, Jr. (1975) "The effects of laws on divorce in American states." Journal of Marriage and the Family 37: 537-547.

STRONG, B. and C. DeVAULT (1986) The Marriage and Family Experience. St. Paul, MN: West.

STRONG, B., S. WILSON, M. ROBBINS, and T. JOHNS (1981) Human sexuality: Essentials. St. Paul, MN: West.

SUAREZ, J., N. WESTON, and N. HARTSTERN (1978) "Mental health interventions in divorce proceedings." American Journal of Orthopsychiatry 48: 273-283.

SYLVAN, I. (1982) "Completing expense forms for modification of support." Family Advocate 4: 12-17.

TAKAS, M. (February, 1986) "Divorce: who gets the blame in 'no-fault'?" Ms. Magazine, p. 48.

TEACHMAN, J. (1983) "Early marriage, premarital fertility, and marital dissolution: results for Blacks and Whites." Journal of Family Issues 4: 105-126.

THIBAUT, J. W. and H. H. KELLEY (1959) The Social Psychology of Groups. New York: John Wiley.

THORNTON, A. (1978) "Marital instability differences and interactions: insights from multivariate contingency tables." Sociology and Social Research 62: 572-595.

THORNTON, A. (1985) "Changing attitudes toward separation and divorce: Causes and consequences." American Journal of Sociology 90: 856-872.

THURNHER, M., C. B. FENN, J. MELICHAR, and D. A. CHIRIBOGA (1983) "Sociodemographics: perspectives on reasons for divorce." Journal of Divorce 6: 25-35.

TILLING, T. (1980) "Your $250,000 baby." Parents 55: 83-87.

TRAFFORD, A. (1982) Crazy Time. New York: Harper & Row.

TYIERE, L. and R. PEACOCK (1982) Learning to Leave. Chicago: Warner.

UDRY, J. R. (1981) "Marital alternatives and marital disruption." Journal of Marriage and the Family 43: 889-897.

United Nations (1985) Demographic Yearbook. New York: United Nations.

U.S. Bureau of the Census (1979) "Current population reports," Series P-23, No. 84, Divorce Child Custody and Child Support. Washington, DC: Government Printing Office.

U.S. Bureau of the Census (1983a) "Current population reports," Series P-23, No. 130, Population Profile of the United States. Washington, DC: Government Printing Office.

U.S. Bureau of the Census (1983b) "Current population reports," Series P-23, No. 124, Child Support and Alimony: 1981. Washington, DC: Government Printing Office.

U.S. Department of Health, Education, and Welfare Public Health Service (1976) "Differentials in health characteristics by marital status: United States, 1971-1972," Series 10, No. 1011 DHEW Pub. No. (HRA) 76-1531.

WAITE, L. J., G. W. HAGGSTROM, and D. E. KANOUSE (1985) "The consequences of parenthood for the marital stability of young adults." American Sociological Review 50: 850-857.

WALLER, W. (1951) The Family: A Dynamic Interpretation. New York: Holt, Rinehart, & Winston. (Originally published, 1938.)

WALLERSTEIN, J. S. (1984) "Children of divorce: preliminary report from a ten-year follow-up of young children." American Journal of Orthopsychiatry 54: 444-460.

WALLERSTEIN, J. S. (1985) "The overburdened child: some long-term consequences of divorce." Social Work 30: 116-123.

WALLERSTEIN, J. S. (1986) "Women after divorce: preliminary report from a ten-year follow-up." American Journal of Orthopsychiatry 56: 65-77.

WALLERSTEIN, J. S. and J. B. KELLEY (1977) "Divorce counseling: a community service for families in the midst of divorce." American Journal of Orthopsychiatry 47: 4-22.

WALLERSTEIN, J. S. and J. B. KELLEY (1980) Surviving the Breakup: How Children and Parents Cope with Divorce. New York: Basic Books.

WEINGARTEN, H. R. (1985) "Marital status and well-being: a national study comparing first-married, currently divorced, and remarried adults." Journal of Marriage and the Family 47: 235-247.

WEINGLASS, J., K. KRESSEL, and M. DEUTSCH (1978) "The role of clergy in divorce: an exploratory survey." Journal of Divorce 2: 57-82.

WEISS, R. S. (1975) Marital Separation. New York: Basic Books.

WEISS, R. S. (1979) Going It Alone: The Family Life and Social Situation of the Single Parent. New York: Basic Books.

WEISS, R. S. (1979) "Issues in the adjudication of custody when parents separate," in G. Levinger and O. C. Moles (eds.) Divorce and Separation: Context, Causes, and Consequences. New York: Basic Books.

WEISS, R. S. (1984) "The impact of marital dissolution on income and consumption in single-parent households." Journal of Marriage and the Family 46: 115-127.

WEISS, W. W. and H. B. COLLADA (1977) "Conciliation counseling: the court's effective mechanism for resolving visitation and custody disputes." Family Co-ordinator 26: 444-458.

WEITZMAN, L. J. (1981) The Marriage Contract: Spouses, Lovers, and the Law. New York: Free Press.

WEITZMAN, L. J. (1985) The Divorce Revolution: The Unexpected Social and Economic Consequences for Women and Children in America. New York: Free Press.

WEITZMAN, L. J. and R. B. DIXON (1979) "Child custody awards: legal standards and empirical patterns for child custody, support and visitation after divorce." UCD Law Review 12: 472-521.

WEITZMAN, L. J. and R. B. DIXON (1980) "The alimony myth: does no-fault make a difference? Family Law Quarterly 14: 141-185.

WELCH, C. E. and S. PRICE-BONHAM (1983) "A decade of no-fault divorce revisted: California, Georgia, and Washington." Journal of Marriage and the Family 45: 411-418.

WHEELER, M. (1974) No-Fault Divorce. Boston: Beacon.

WHITE, S. W. and B. L. BLOOM (1981) "Factors related to the adjustment of divorcing men." Family Relations 30: 349-360.

WHITESIDE, M. F. (1982) "Remarriage: a family developmental process." Journal of Marital and Family Therapy 8: 59-68.

WISEMAN, R. S. (1975) "Crisis theory and the process of divorce." Social Casework 56: 205-212.

WOODARD, J. C., J. ZABEL, and C. DeCOSTA (1980) "Loneliness and divorce." Journal of Divorce 4: 73-82.

WRIGHT, D. (1985) "Revitalizing the social exchange model of divorce." Unpublished paper.

WRIGHT, D. W. and S. J. PRICE (1986) "Court-ordered support payments: the effect of the former-spouse relationship on compliance." Journal of Marriage and the Family 48: 869-874.

WRIGHT, G. C. and D. M. STETSON (1978) "The impact of no-fault divorce law reform on divorce in American States." Journal of Marriage and the Family 40: 575-580.

"Young adult children face major problems upon parental divorce." (May, 1986) Marriage and Divorce Today, pp. 1-2.

YOUNG, J. J. (1978) "The divorced Catholics movement." Journal of Divorce 2: 83-97.

ZEISS, A. M., R. A. ZEISS, and S. M. JOHNSON (1980) "Sex differences in initiation and adjustment to divorce." Journal of Divorce 4: 21-33.

AUTHOR INDEX

Abarbanel, A., 88
Adams, B. N., 9, 19, 20
Agopian, M. W., 104
Ahrons, C. R., 7, 47, 58, 67, 68, 69, 71
Alan Guttmacher Institute, 17
Albrecht, S. L., 21, 34, 43, 57, 64
Anderson, E. A., 66
Anspach, D. F., 47
Anthony, E. J., 75, 76, 84
Arendell, T., 122
Asher, S. J., 55, 58, 59, 60, 61, 65
Atkin, E., 85
Ayers, G. W., 135

Bahr, H. M., 64
Bahr, S. J., 24
Ballentine, C., 83
Balswick, J. O., 18, 41, 58
Bane, M. J., 73
Bardwick, J., 63
Barringer, K. D., 49, 56, 65, 66, 67
Becker, G. S., 22, 30
Bell, R. R., 24
Bem, S., 45
Benedek, E. P., 136, 137
Benedek, R. S., 136, 137
Beninger, E. S., 62, 111
Berardo, D. H., 65
Berardo, F. M., 16, 23, 40
Berke, M. A., 71
Berman, W. H., 58, 59, 62, 65, 69
Bernard, A. M., 21
Bernard, J., 64
Bernstein, B. E., 108
Blackwell, R., 115
Blake, N. M., 9
Blisk, D., 89
Block, M. R., 18
Blood, R. O., Jr., 23, 26, 28, 30
Bloom, B. L., 7, 31, 33, 34, 36, 37, 38, 39, 45, 46, 51, 55, 58, 59, 60, 61, 64, 65, 69, 83
Bohannan, P., 41, 42, 47, 48, 107
Bonham, J., 115, 116
Booth, A., 23
Bould, S., 66
Bowlby, J., 46
Bowman, M. E., 47
Brandwein, R. A., 52, 62, 122
Brown, C. A., 52, 59, 62
Brown, E. M., 49, 108, 126, 127
Brown, P., 39, 44, 61, 62, 63, 67, 69, 131, 132
Brown, T., 87
Brown-Wilson, K., 65
Buehler, C. A., 59
Bumpass, L. L., 25, 26, 27, 28
Burgess, E. W., 23, 26
Burr, W. R., 25

Caldwell, R. A., 36, 37, 38, 39, 51, 64
Camara, K. A., 78, 80, 89
Campbell, A., 122
Carter, H., 24, 25, 26, 36, 37, 59
Casto, R. F., 44, 46, 48, 62, 66, 69, 99
Cedrone, A. R., 36, 37, 38, 39, 51
Chambers, T. K., 114, 119, 120
Cheng, C. K., 25
Cherlin, A. J., 12, 30, 31, 36, 37, 38, 99
Chester, R., 10, 42
Chiriboga, D. A., 33, 34, 42, 43, 44, 45, 64, 65, 66, 126
Clark, H., 91
Clement, C., 45
Cleveland, M., 64, 70
Cline, D., 84
Coane, J., 137
Coho, A., 125
Collada, H. B., 131
Combs, E. R., 110, 111
Converse, P. E., 122
Coogler, O. J., 133, 134
Coombs, L. C., 24, 26, 28
Corcoran, M., 121
Cottrell, L. S., 26
Cox, M., 55, 58, 59, 62, 65, 70, 74, 77, 78, 79, 80, 83, 84, 85, 86, 89
Cox, R., 55, 58, 59, 62, 65, 70, 74, 77, 78, 79, 80, 83, 84, 85, 86, 89
Crosby, J. F., 8
Cuber, J. F., 21, 23, 49
Cutler, L., 42, 66
Cutright, P., 18, 29

Dahl, B. B., 100, 101, 103, 112
Davidson, J. L., 18
Deckert, P., 64
DeCosta, C., 64
DeFrain, J., 62
Demos, J., 11
Derdeyn, A. P., 92, 93
DeShane, M. R., 65
Despert, J., 74
Deutsch, M., 68, 71, 84, 125, 127, 130, 135
DeVault, C., 26
Dixon, R. B., 40, 66, 98, 99, 100, 101, 121
Dreyfus, E. A., 64
Dyer, E. D., 9

Eden, P., 114, 115, 116
Edwards, C. S., 114, 117, 118
Edwards, J. N., 23
Eirick, R., 62
Eisler, R. T., 113, 115
Elkin, M., 91, 92, 97, 131, 136
England, J. L., 14, 15, 70
Eshleman, J. R., 16, 26, 27, 28

Esman, A. H., 89
Espenshade, T., 114
Fain, H. M., 100
Federico, J., 40
Feld, A. L., 111
Feldberg, R., 58
Felton, D. J., 39, 44, 69
Fenelon, B., 17
Fenn, C. B., 33, 34
Ferguson, D., 87
Fine, M. A., 85
Fisher, E. O., 126, 127
Flynn, C., 102, 103
Fox, E. M., 52, 62
Fox, H., 58, 61, 62
Freed, D. J., 27, 94-96, 102
Friedman, H. J., 85
Froiland, D. J., 41, 42, 75, 76
Furstenberg, F., 17, 49, 86, 89

Galligan, R. J., 24
Gardner, R. A., 88
Geerkin, M., 60
Gelles, R. J., 104
Gettleman, S., 10, 11
Glaudin, V., 23
Glenn, N. D., 16, 17, 18, 76
Glick, P. C., 24, 25, 26, 28, 36, 37, 59, 69, 71, 73, 82
Goetting, A., 58, 61
Goldman, J., 138
Goldsmith, J., 67, 68, 71
Goode, W. J., 7, 11, 23, 31, 32, 40, 43, 45, 46, 48, 49, 57, 58, 60, 62, 65, 109
Goodman, K. L., 64
Gove, W. R., 59, 60, 61, 62, 63, 64
Grambs, J. D., 18
Grant, 71
Granvold, D. K., 56, 63, 127
Gray, G. M., 60
Green, R. G., 23, 34
Groeneveld, L. R., 29, 30, 128
Gubrium, J. F., 66
Guerney, L., 136
Gunter, B. C., 27, 100

Hackney, H., 22
Haggstrom, G. W., 27
Hajal, F., 138
Halem, L. C., 101, 136
Hampe, G. D., 47
Hannan, M. T., 29
Hanson, S., 47, 48, 49, 56
Harmelink, P. J., 111
Harroff, P. B., 21, 23, 39
Hartstern, N., 68
Haynes, J. M., 133
Herrman, M. S., 135
Herzog, E., 89

Hess, R. D., 78, 80, 89
Hetherington, E. M., 7, 55, 58, 59, 62, 65, 70, 77, 78, 79, 80, 81, 82, 83, 84, 85, 86, 89
Hicks, M. W., 22
Hill, R., 15
Hodges, W. F., 36, 37, 38, 39, 46, 51, 65, 83
Hogan, M. J., 59
Holmes, T., 55, 58
Holmes, W. M., 51, 52
Honig, M., 29
Houseknecht, S. K., 30
Hozman, T. L., 41, 42, 75
Huber, J., 27
Hunt, B., 34, 45, 55, 70, 108
Hunt, M., 34, 45, 55, 70, 108
Hutter, M., 9
Hyatt, R., 47
Hynes, W. J., 67

Irving, H. H., 133

Jacobson, D. S., 75, 79, 85
Jaffe, B., 84
Joffe, W., 127
Johns, T., 23
Johnson, D., 23, 100
Johnson, E. S., 47, 48
Johnson, J. S., 43, 52, 61, 65, 66
Johnson, M. P., 30
Johnson, S. M., 62
Johnson, W. D., 50, 110
Jones, F. N., 89
Jordan, L., 136
Juhasy, A. M., 42

Kanouse, D. E., 27
Kaslow, F., 31, 47
Kelley, H. H., 22
Kelly, J. B., 7, 44, 45, 63, 68, 74, 75, 76, 77, 78, 79, 80, 81, 82, 84, 86, 88, 119, 122, 136, 137, 138, 139
Kephart, W. M., 25
Kessler, S., 31, 41, 42, 43, 56, 57, 63, 66, 128
Kimura, Y., 25
Kindle, K. R., 69
Kitson, G. C., 7, 32, 33, 34, 36, 37, 38, 39, 45, 51, 52, 55, 67, 69
Kohen, J. A., 58
Korman, S. K., 93, 97
Krantzler, M., 43, 44, 45, 46, 49, 51, 63, 69, 70, 124
Kraus, S., 41, 58, 59, 61
Kressel, K., 58, 68, 71, 84, 125, 126, 127, 129, 134
Kubler-Ross, E., 75
Kunz, P. R., 14, 15, 21
Kurdek, L. A., 79, 80, 89
Kurtz, P. M., 109

Lachman, M. E., 43, 57
Ladbrook, D., 60
Landes, E. M., 24, 30

Landis, J. T., 21, 74
Langelier, R., 64
Langlie, J. K., 37, 51, 52
Lasch, C., 92
Lavoie, R. 111
Lerner, M., 73
Leslie, E. M., 18, 100
Leslie, G. R., 15, 18, 23, 93, 97, 100
Levinger, G., 7, 22, 23, 32, 33, 34, 48, 51, 52
Levy, T. M., 127
Lewis, R. A., 21, 22, 23, 25, 26, 28, 29
Locke, H. J., 23
Longfellow, C., 74, 82
Lopez-Morillas, M., 125, 134
Lowenthal, M. C., 66
Lowery, C. R., 77, 80, 85, 89
Luckey, E., 23
Luepnitz, D. A., 89
Lynch, J. J., 59

Magrab, P. R., 74, 80
Manela, R., 39, 44, 63, 69, 130, 131
Markowitz, J., 10, 11
Marroni, E., 65, 67
Mason, P. R., 34
McCubbin, H., 100, 101, 103, 112
McDermott, J. F., 78, 79, 136
McDonald, M., 117
McKenry, P. C., 135, 137
Melichar, J., 33, 34, 44
Menaghan, E. G., 60
Mendes, H. A., 62, 87
Michael, R. T., 24, 30
Miller, M. H., 25
Minuchin, S., 67
Mitchell, K., 63
Moir, R. N., 34
Moller, A. S., 25
Monahan, T. P., 25, 39
Moore, S. F., 24, 27, 121
Moorman, J. W., 17
Moreland, J., 74, 85
Mott, F. L., 24, 27, 121
Mueller, C. W., 28, 29
Murdock, G. P., 9, 10
Murstein, B., 23
Myers, J. C., 65

National Center for Health Statistics, 17, 19, 59
Nelson, G., 64
Niles, R. L., 31, 33, 34
Nord, C. W., 89
Norton, A. J., 17, 28, 73, 87
Nye, F. I., 23, 40, 74

Oakland, T., 93, 100, 101, 102, 113
O'Gorman, H. J., 134
Orthner, D. K., 87

Pais, J., 65, 66
Parke, R. D., 82

Parkes, C. M., 69
Peacock, R., 39
Pearlin, L. I., 43, 52, 58, 61, 65, 66
Pearson, J., 133
Pedler, L. M., 56, 63
Pett, M. G., 66, 67
Pittman, J., 62
Platt, M., 22
Pope, H., 28, 29
Price, S. J., 67, 119
Price-Bonham, S., 18, 41, 58, 62, 69, 99, 115, 116, 121

Rachofsky, M., 134
Rahe, R., 55, 58
Raschke, H., 17, 19, 36, 39, 48, 49, 55, 56, 62, 63, 65, 66, 67, 74, 89
Raschke, V. J., 89
Renne, K., 59
Rheinstein, M., 11
Rice, D. G., 67, 126
Risman, B. J., 87
Robbins, M., 23
Roberts, J., 45, 64, 125
Roberts, T. W., 67
Robertson, N., 9
Rodgers, R. H., 71
Rodgers, W. L., 121
Rose, V. L., 58, 69
Rosenberg, E. B., 137
Ross, H., 18, 24, 27, 46, 79
Rubin, E., 85
Rutter, M., 74

Sabalis, R. F., 135
Salts, C. J., 41, 42, 43, 130
Santrock, J. W., 87
Sawhill, I. V., 18, 24, 30, 49, 82
Scanzoni, J., 11, 12, 18, 22, 29
Scheillic, S., 56, 63
Schooner, C., 58
Schulman, G. L., 68
Schwebel, A., 74, 85
Seagull, A. A., 85
Seagull, E. A., 85
Seal, K., 110, 111, 114, 121
Settle, S. A., 77, 80, 86, 89
Shelton, B. S., 17
Shields, L., 121
Shurtz, N. E., 111
Siesky, A. E., 79, 81, 89
Skeen, P., 137
Smart, L. S., 56
Smith, C. E., 25
Smith, J. S., 111
Sonne, J. C., 132
Sorensen, A., 118
South, S. J., 24, 24, 27
Spanier, G. B., 7, 21, 22, 23, 25, 26, 28, 29, 30, 33, 39, 40, 43, 44, 46, 47, 48, 49, 56, 57, 62, 66, 69, 70, 99

Spicer, J. W., 47
Spitze, G., 24, 27, 30
Sporakowski, M. J., 23, 34
Sprenkle, D. H., 132, 134
Stack, S., 60
Stein, J. A., 45, 64, 125
Steinman, S., 88
Stetson, D. M., 27, 99
Storm, C. L., 132, 134
Strong, B., 23, 26
Suarez, J., 68
Sudia, C. E., 89
Suspanic, M., 17, 18, 51, 52
Sussman, M. B., 32, 33
Sweet, J. A., 25, 26, 27, 28
Sylvan, I., 116
Systra, L., 36, 37, 38, 39, 51
Szinovacz, M., 22

Tachman, C., 84
Takas, M., 107
Tatcher, A. M., 31, 33, 34
Teachman, J., 19
Thibaut, J. W., 22
Thompson, 21
Thornton, A., 25, 26, 27
Thurnher, M., 33, 34, 45, 66
Tilling, T., 114
Trafford, A., 8, 52
Triere, L., 39
Tuma, N. B., 29, 30
Turk, D. C., 58, 59, 62, 65

Udry, J. R., 31
U.S. Bureau of the Census, 18, 73, 82, 109, 112, 113, 117, 123
U.S. Department of HEW, 59

Vanderkooi, L., 133
Vess, J. D., 74, 85
Vinick, B. H., 47, 48

Waite, L. J., 27
Walker, T. B., 27, 94-96, 102

Waller, W., 7, 41
Wallerstein, J. S., 7, 44, 45, 62, 63, 64, 65, 68, 74, 75, 76, 77, 78, 79, 80, 81, 82, 84, 86, 88, 119, 136, 137, 138, 139
Wallin, P., 23
Wallisch, L. S., 67, 68, 71
Warshak, R. A., 87
Watson, C., 84
Weber, R. E., 135
Wechsler, R. C., 83
Weingarten, H. R., 58
Weinglass, J., 125, 130, 135
Weiss, R. S., 31, 37, 42, 43, 44, 45, 46, 47, 48, 49, 50, 51, 52, 55, 58, 60, 62, 64, 69, 70, 84, 85, 100, 107, 123
Weiss, W. W., 131
Weitzman, L. J., 7, 12, 40, 66, 91, 92, 98, 100, 101, 102, 108, 109, 110, 111, 112, 113, 114, 117, 119, 120, 121, 122
Welch, C. E., 99, 121
Welch, G. J., 127
Westman. J., 84
Weston, N., 68
Wheeler, M., 97-98
White, P., 65, 66
White, S. W., 55, 58, 59, 60, 61, 64, 65
Whiteman, V., 39, 44, 69
Whiteside, M. F., 75
Wilson, S., 23
Wiseman, R. S., 41, 42
Wolfe, D. M., 23, 26, 30
Woodard, J. C., 64
Wright, D. W., 22, 52, 62, 119
Wright, G. C., 27, 99
Yamamura, D. S., 25
Young, J. J., 26, 129
Zabel, J., 64
Zeiss, A. M., 62
Zeiss, R. A., 62
Zongker, C. E., 129
Zumeta, Z., 24, 26, 28

SUBJECT INDEX

Adjustment to divorce: anger, 56; areas of, 56; coparenting, 71; depression, 56-57; former spouse relationship, 67-71; men and women, 62-66; mental health, 60; mourning, 56-57; personality characteristics, 67; physical health, 59-60; positive aspects, 57-58, process, 55-56; psychological resources, 67; recovery, 57; reasons for problems, 60-64; related factors, 65-67; sex-role attitudes, 63; stressors, 58-59
Adjustment to separation: attachment to spouse, 46; duration of marriage, 44; sex-role attitudes, 45; stages, 43-44; time, 44

Adversary system: duration of marriage, 44; sex-role attitudes, 45; stages, 43-44; time, 44
Age: age-specific divorce rate, 14; children and child support, 114-116; children's response to divorce, 78-79; relation to divorce rate, 17; variation in divorce rate, 15
Alimony: adversary system, 93, 97; criteria, 112; function, 112; history, 111; male eligibility, 113
Alternatives to marriage: economic resources, 29; education, 30; employment opportunities, 30; sources of affection, 31; welfare, 29
Assets in marriage: see Marital property

Attorneys: adversary system, 91; impact of no-fault, 99; therapeutic role, 134-135; typology, 135
Attractions to marriage: age, 25; companionship, 23; education, 21-22; employment, 24; esteem for spouse, 23; home ownership, 24; income, 23; marital quality, 23; race, 25; religion, 25; sexual pleasure, 23

Baby boom cohort, 19
Barriers to divorce: children, 27; community, 28; economic, 27-28, home ownership, 24; legal, 27; marital bond, 28; parental divorce, 28-29; previous marriage, 28; religiosity, 26
"Best interests of the child" doctrine, 92-93, 104

Child custody: joint, 88, 102-103; primary role, 87, 101-102; sole, 87, 101-102; split, 87, 102; "tender years" doctrine, 101-102
Child stealing: motivation, 104-105; Parental Kidnapping Prevention Act, 105; rates, 104; Uniform Child Custody Jurisdiction Act, 105
Child support: adequacy, 113-114; age of child, 115-116; amount, 113; calculation, 113-114; children's expenses, 115-116; compliance, 117-119; enforcement, 109; cost of child rearing, 114; and inflation, 114-117; parental contribution, 114; self-starting system, 119
Child Support Enforcement Amendment, 119-120
Children: activities with, 68; depression, 74-77; intervention with, 125, 136-139; legal rights, 104; news of divorce, 74; parental conflict during separation, 80-81; parenting during separation, 80-81; perceptions, 75; predivorce family relations, 79-80; rates, 73; social support, 81; somatic disturbances, 76; temperament, 79; variations in response by sex, 78-79
Clergy, 81, 130
Conciliation courts, 131-132

Divorce counseling: contrasted with therapy, 125-127; defined, 126-127; group approaches, 128-129; theories and strategies, 127-128
Divorce rates: age, 17; children involved, 73; duration of marriage, 17; escape valve theory, 9; European, 9-10; financial stability, 24; measurement, 12-15; Moslem, 9-11; no-fault legislation, 99-100; non-European, 9-10; political instability/war, 10-12; present rate, 19; race, 17, 19; refined divorce rate, 14-15; region, 17; religion, 18-19; rural/urban, 17; SES, 18; standardized divorce rate, 14; state of economy, 15-16
Economic consequences of divorce: displaced homemakers, 120-121; employment of women, 121-122; IRS, 40; older women, 122; role overload, 122; stress, 122; welfare, 122
Economics: in adjustment, 66; alimony, 111-113; as alternative to marriage, 29; as barrier to

divorce, 27-28; child custody, 87-88; child support, 113-120; consequences of divorce, 120-123; as issue in divorce, 18, 107; marital property, 108-111; postdivorce income, 109; single-parent family, 82-83
Education: attorneys, 136; form of group intervention, 128
Exchange theory, 21-22

Family: extended and children, 81; reaction, 47-48, 81; returning home, 49; sibling reaction, 48; support, 48; telling about separation, 47
Fathers: child custody, 73, 87, 100-101; compliance with child support, 116-119; history of role in divorce legislation, 91-93; parenting during separation, 80-81; single-parent families, 83-85; visitation, 86-87
Former spouse relationships, 67-71; coparenting relationship, 68; distrust, 70-71; nonparenting, 69-71; sex, 70; typology, 71
Friends: reaction, 50; stages in response, 50-51; telling about separation, 46, 49

Grounds for divorce: adversary system, 93-97
Grandparents, 104
Guardian ad litem, 104

Health problems: explanations for, 60-61; mental health and divorce, 60; physical health and divorce, 59-60; somatic disturbances in children, 76; suicide, 59-60
History of divorce: Church of England, 10; divorce legislation, 91-93; feminism, 11; marital property, 109-110; U.S., 10-12

Intervention: approaches, 126; attorney therapeutic role, 134-135; clergy, 129; conciliation courts, 130-131; consumer, 125; counseling, 125-126; mediation, 131-134; group approaches, 127-129; services for children, 135-138; traditional philosophy, 124

Joint custody: legal, 88, 102-103; physical, 88, 103

Marital property: assets, 110-112; definition, 109; division, 109-110
Maternal preference doctrine: see "Tender years" doctrine
Men: adjustment to divorce, 64; compliance with child support, 116-120; custody, 73, 87, 101-103; involvement with children, 69; reaction to separation, 45; reasons for separation/divorce, 32-34; returning home, 47; sex expectations, 23-24; similarity to women in response to divorce, 62; single-parent families, 83-85; telling friends, 49-50
Mothers: parenting during separation, 80-81; role in history of divorce legislation, 91-92; single-parent families, 82-85
Mourning: reaction of children, 75-76; stage in adjustment, 56-57

No-fault: displaced homemakers, 99; divorce rate, 99-100; grounds, 97; role of attorneys, 98; role reversal in filing, 100

Parent Locater Service, 105, 119
Parental Kidnapping Prevention Act, 105

Race: attraction to marriage, 25; difference in adjustment, 63; influence on divorce rate, 18; separation, 38
Reasons for divorce, 31-34; complaints, 32; major factors, 29-34
Reconciliation: consequences of, 52-53; couple characteristics, 51-52; explanation, 52; rates, 51
Religion: as attraction to marriage, 25; as barrier to divorce, 26; influence on divorce rate, 18-19; role in adjustment, 67

Separation: adjustment to, 43-46; attachment to spouse, 46; bargaining, 40; children, 74-81; decision, 39-41; emotional impact, 42-46; frequency, 36-37; function of, 38-39; length, 39-40; men, 32-34, 45; parenting during separation, 80; precursor to divorce, 38-39; physical, 42-43; racial differences, 38; reasons, 29-32, 44-45; reconciliation, 51-53; repeated, 37-38; stages, 41-43; telling friends, family, 46-50; women, 32-34, 45
Separation distress: children's response, 74-81; duration of marriage, 44; expected vs. unexpected, 44; impact of time, 44; related to who initiated, 43-44; sex-role attitudes, 45; telling children, 75

Sex: as attraction to marriage, 23; difference between men and women, 23-24; former spouse, 70
Single-parent families: changes in parenting, 84-85; effect on child development, 88-89; fathers, 83-84, 89; long-term impact, 89; loneliness, 82-84; mothers, 82-83; postdivorce conflict, 84; rates, 73; role overload, 82; stress, 82; visitation, 85-87
Social support: for children, 81; church, 81, 130; co-workers, 50; family, 48, 104; friends, 49-50; groups, 128-130; women, 64
Stages of divorce: disillusionment, 41; erosion, 41-42; physical separation, 42-43; mourning, 56; recovery, 57

"Tender years doctrine," 100-102
Typology: attorneys, 134; former spouse relationships, 71

Uniform Marriage and Divorce Act, 104

Visitation: fathers, 85-87; frequency and sex of child, 86; grandparents, 104

Welfare: alternative to marriage, 29; consequence of divorce, 123
Women: adjustment to divorce, 62-66; alternatives to marriage, 30; positive aspects of divorce, 63; older, 120-121; postdivorce economic status, 120-123; reasons for separation, 32-34; returning home, 47; role overload, 82-83, 122; separated, 40, 45; sex-role attitudes, 45; single-parent families, 82-85; social differences and adjustment, 63

ABOUT THE AUTHORS

Sharon J. Price (Ph.D., Iowa State University) is Professor of Child and Family Development and Sociology at the University of Georgia. She has authored over 50 publications in the areas of divorce, remarriage, fathers, marital adjustment, marital interaction, and parent-child relationships. She is past president of the National Council on Family Relations, American Council on Education Fellow in the Administrative Leadership program, and recipient of the Osborne Award for Outstanding Teaching in the area of the family (presented by the National Council on Family Relations). She lectures widely and has appeared on national and regional television shows.

Patrick C. McKenry (Ph.D., University of Tennessee, Postdoctoral Fellow, University of Georgia) is Professor of Family Relations and Human Development, Ohio State University. He has authored more than 40 publications in the areas of marital dissolution, marital interaction, and parent-child relationships. He presently serves on the editorial boards of *Family Relations, Family Perspective,* and *Family Science Review.*